ON THE RIGHT LINES

FOOTPLATE MEMORIES
by
BERT STEWART

PETER WATTS
Publishing

ISBN 0 906025 34 6

First published 1982
Reprinted 1987
by
Peter Watts Publishing Ltd
Stag House, Gydynap Lane
Inchbrook, Woodchester
Gloucestershire GL5 5EZ

Typeset by Washington Printing, Cheltenham
Printed by Trio Graphics, Gloucester

Front cover:
Full cry on Shap! Former L.M.S. 'Jubilee' class 6P 4-6-0 no. 45601 'British Guiana'
attacks the northbound climb of the famous bank un-assisted and is portrayed passing
Shap Wells in July 1963. *(Eric Cope/Colour-Rail)*

CONTENTS

Bert Stewart stands proudly with his beloved 'Blue Lady'.
(Photograph courtesy of Chorley Guardian)

FOREWORD

by

DAVID SHEPHERD

The end of steam on our railways in 1968 saw not only the end of a wonderfully exciting era, but something deep and fundamental also went out of the lives of the great multitude of true railwaymen—men with a family tradition of railway service who were born and bred in the very air of the great steam sheds.

These were the 'characters' whose like will never be seen again. They belong perhaps to a more romantic age, but nevertheless this was a time when one was not afraid of hard work. Grime, bad pay, long hours were an accepted part of that hard work because pride was still a word that meant something.

Such a character is Bert Stewart who came into my life at about 6.30 am on the morning of April 6th 1967, in the gloomy depths of a rapidly decaying Crewe South shed.

I had recently become the proud owner of two steam locomotives—British Rail Class 9F and a BR Standard 4, numbers 92203 and 75029. They were outside the shed in the light of early morning, with a full head of steam, about to begin their two day journey down to Longmoor, through London.

Bert was taking the first turn on the Standard 9, and we had a riot of fun on that journey. I was kept entertained with a continuous flow of stories, some repeatable, most hilarious, as we thundered down the mainline. I realised that Bert, like so many of the real steam characters whom I have been privileged to meet since, had steam in his blood.

I was to meet Bert once more while he was still working for British Rail. I had been given a footplate pass on an Inter-City Electric from Crewe to Euston and return. Bert of course was driving. What a journey that was. And I have a movie to prove it. The Inspector concerned is safe in his anonymity, but we did have fun as I took the controls and touched 104 miles per hour through Watford! But it could never be quite the same as the good old days of steam.

Thanks however to the Bert Stewarts of this world, the memories are kept alive for those now growing up in a more impersonal and functional age, when romance doesn't seem to count for anything anymore.

David Shepherd.

Chapter I
EVERY BOY WANTS TO BE ONE

Like any other Lancashire lad of the ripe old age of seven years, my favourite summer game was cricket. Along with my pals I used to play endless games, doubtless sometimes to the annoyance of the neighbours. With a broken bat, sometimes merely a strip torn off an orange box, a chalked wicket on a convenient brick wall or wooden fence, and a battered old tennis ball, we would dream of partnering Len Hutton against Don Bradman's team. I am sure that many of these childhood 'Test stars' also dreamed of battling in the modern version of the 'Wars of the Roses' against Len Hutton!

But my dreams were different. Despite my regrets at having to miss a game of cricket, I had a greater purpose. I had an appointment with the Gods. To the echoes of a screamed "Howzat?" I would wander off to my favourite spot, my little corner of Heaven, known to other mortals as Bradshaw Field.

It was a pleasant place to be, sat on the embankment among the daisies, mountain lupins, and the straggling vines of convolvulus. High in the bright blue summer sky birds wheeled, glided and plunged, weaving a black network of flight through the lazy plumes of smoke rising from the factory chimneys. As far as I was concerned, no breath of wind ever disturbed the peace of this miniature paradise overlooking Adlington Junction.

Even at the early age of seven years my mind was made up. I had decided. I would someday be an engine driver. The only toys I ever wanted were train sets, clockwork Hornby locos to race dizzily round circular tracks of pressed tinplate. Railway engines were my main interest in life, and at all moments in my spare time I could be found down at Bradshaw Field.

Filled with excited envy, as I lay on the grassy bank, I would watch the trains go by, some resplendent in their claret livery of the London, Midland & Scottish Railway, others in the red lined black of the old Lancashire & Yorkshire. Through the wraiths of sooty smoke (the strange and pungent smell still turns me on!) I waved at the crews; I became such a part of the railway scenery that footplatemen would look for me, greeting me with carolling shrieks from the polished brass whistles. I was in ecstacy. Who were these blue-overalled, black capped heroes who rode the mighty Iron Horses? Where did they come from, and where did they go?

I was determined to find the answers to these and many more questions. For some of these questions the answers lay many long and impatient years ahead.

I was rather fortunate in that I became friendly with two drivers who, between them, fanned the flames of my childhood ambition as surely and as expertly as any 'passed fireman'. One lived quite close to my home in Adlington, the other lived in Fleetwood, where I was taken for summer holidays in the early 1930's. Of course, I used to think that they were kings, at the very least.

In those days pocket-money was not quite so plentiful as now, and in order to buy railway magazines and toys I had to find an extra source of revenue. After much discussion with my parents—"You've got to get yourself up, Sundays as well" and "You'll need to be in bed early at night to get your sleep in"—I was allowed to have a newspaper round.

I soon became acclimatized to the early hours, although some mornings, especially when it rained and I had to be down at the railway station before 6.00 am to meet the newspaper train, I wished that there was an easier way to earn pocket money. But I soon found a bonus in this particular duty which made me oblivious to such trifles as weather. The driver of the newspaper train finished his shift at Adlington. While I was busy collecting my newsagent employer's daily quota, he would climb down from the footplate and start his walk for home. Frequently, I would excitedly pester him with questions and become so engrossed that I would completely forget my bundle of newspapers!

To say that it was love at first sight, is not too much, if any, of an exaggeration. The feeling that I had for this driver is inexplicable—the nearest description is adoration. A mutual bond sprang up between us in our love of railways, steam locomotives in particular. He accepted me for what I then was, a young lad tremendously interested in the footplate life. The only difference now is that I am a little older.

Shortly after I had discovered my new-found friend, the school holidays began, and as usual, I made my way down to my favourite spot in the Bradshaw Field. I was particularly fascinated by the operations in the shunting yard at Adlington Junction, and eagerly awaited the arrival of the shunting engine.

Amid a billowing cloud of white smoke and a series of calls on the whistle, answered by some other locos in the yard, it arrived for the day's duty. And who should be the driver but my friend, Mr. Birchall. My day was made, or so I thought. But when he invited me onto his footplate I was speechless. Me, a steam-engine daft lad, actually standing on the footplate in front of the firebox! To describe my excitement as I handled the controls is impossible, but I can see that cab as clearly as if I were standing there now. The fireman on that Lancashire & Yorkshire Class 5 tender locomotive even allowed me to shovel some coal into the open grate. I doubt if my efforts did much for the boiler pressure, but they certainly got me all steamed up and excited.

My other engine-driver friend actually lived, of all places, at the boarding house where we stayed for our summer holidays. I cannot remember now exactly how it was that I first knew about Alf Beck being an engine-driver, but more than likely, I happened to be around as he came off duty. As soon as we arrived at that house in Bramley Avenue, I would be excitedly dashing around—"Where is he?"—"Where has he gone?"—"Will he be home soon?", and a million other questions of a like nature.

As I got to know him and his duty roster a bit better I had no need of these questions. Once arrived, impatient to meet my friend, I would leave my parents to the chore of unpacking, and I was off like the proverbial shot from a gun. Running all the way to the loco sheds was an absolute must. Only by this frantic exercise could I be sure of getting there before Alf left for home. If I could endeavour to meet him before he left the yard, I could be sure that he would take me on a tour of the sheds. Under his watchful but encouraging eye I would clamber on to the engines, living in a fantasy world of main line expresses and night mails to Scotland.

Those sheds were something like a modern preservationist's dream of heaven. Horwich built 'Crabs' stood side by side with Crewe built 'Black 5's' as if guarding the aristocratic 'Jubilees'. Like supporters at a soccer match, there was always a host of the small fish-dock shunters around. It seemed to me that they were always on the boil. I loved them all.

The homeward part of these activities was always the same. As we wended our way to Bramley Avenue, Alf would tell me of his day's work, while I, in open-mouthed wonder would be half-heartedly using his hand-rag in a futile endeavour to cleanse myself of oil and soot. Invariably I would arrive back at the boarding house as black as the ace of spades, to the resigned despair of my Mum and Dad and to the ill-concealed delight of Alf and his wife. Any dirty clothes of mine always appeared freshly laundered next day.

During these holidays I never went near the beach—sand castles were for the kids. My entire time was devoted to the life at Fleetwood Station. I was fascinated watching the boat-trains from the Isle of Man, and the Holiday Specials from London. These latter, as I later found out were developments of the Slip-Coach Expresses which used to set out from Euston, slipping coaches at Nuneaton and Coventry.

If only I could have had a camera in those wonderful days. It is a matter of debate which was the centre of the greatest activity—the station, as the passenger trains disgorged their freight of bustling human beings, or the fish docks as the little shunters snorted and clanked ceaselessly among an absolute maze of wagons. It was quite an education (for which I was later to be grateful I had absorbed) watching those saddle tanks and tender engines perform. They never seemed to stop, marshalling the newly loaded fish wagons ready for distribution throughout the British Isles, or the empty coal wagons for return to the coal-fields of Yorkshire.

By the end of the week I was on first-name terms with most of the drivers and firemen; after a minimum of persuasion on my part, I was allowed to ride on the footplate between the docks and the loco sheds. My role as unofficial crewman made me the envy of many other boys. I helped, in my small but enthusiastic way, during re-coaling and topping-up with water operations. Those engine-men were good to me. I shared their tea and sandwiches, and listened to their conversations. It is no breach of confidence when I revealed that some of the talk was a little more mature than my Mum would have wished her son to hear. But I had a rare old time with those men, and I consider it a privilege to have known them. Most youngsters have their heroes, and I was no exception. The gods on my Mount Olympus were engine-men; I looked up to them, admired them, and hoped that one day I might be chosen to be really one of them.

Dreams are like bubbles—they are liable to burst. In the spring of 1938 I finished my education at the Saint Paul's Church of England School in Adlington. Long before the term ended I was all ready to begin my life as a railwayman. But any ideas I had about riding on the footplate were thwarted by my parents. They had secured for me a job in the spinning room at Cowling Mills in Chorley. I was to become one of the 'cloth cap and clogs' brigade—an honourable trade, but not one of my choosing. It is best to draw a veil over my dismay and intense dislike.

I was duly installed in the spinning room where, at the time, I felt as if I was the rubbing rag for everyone. Of course, my own stubborn disapproval of everything around me did not help. As the factory hooter hastened my reluctant footsteps and the gates swung behind me, I felt a certain sympathy with the prisoners on Dartmoor.

Each dreary day succeeded another, each no different to the one which had gone before. ''Take those bobbin links over to the number three frame.'' ''Get the mashin's ready, lad. Look sharp about it.'' ''Go across to the stores for some cotton waste, and bring the oil-can on your way back.'' ''Fetch this'', ''fetch that'', ''Do the other''. If I had had the time I could have cried with frustration.

And so seemingly endless days passed into weeks and months. But at long last I was able to find blessed relief from this ceaseless drudgery. I did something foolish, morally wrong, something I'd never even done at school. I played truant.

For two, sometimes three days out of the week I would fail to report for duty; instead, I would make my way over to the railway sidings at Yarrow Gate. Here, in the peace of mind which only boyhood fantasies could bring, I sat watching the trains on their various roads to Manchester or Preston or London, or perhaps, I thought, even the other side of the world. But dreams must end, and another bubble was about to burst.

My first few Friday pay-days came and the un-opened pay-packet was handed over to my mother the instant I arrived home. She always seemed puzzled when she checked the coins. ''I wonder why they always pay you short, Herbert'', she would say as she gave me my week's pocket money. Sensing trouble, I made a few attempts to hide the real reason by trying to put the blame on the pay-clerk, or by talking vaguely about 'trial periods of apprenticeship'.

My mother put up with this situation for a little while, until one day she came over to the factory and made a few searching inquiries. As the boss explained patiently and courteously, it was only natural that since I had scarcely worked a full week since I had started employment at the Mill, I should not be paid for a full week's work. My mother was a reasonable woman and accepted this explanation.

My explanation was not so reasonably nor so kindly received. When I arrived home at the end of the day I ran into the full-blown wrath of my Mum and Dad. I told them that I did not like the factory, the people, the work. With my feelings a mixture of fear and bravado, frustration and hope, I begged of them to take me away—I wanted to work on the railway.

After much discussion and argument, both heated and tearful, my father finally relented. He agreed to ask his boss at Lostock Hall if I could enter the railway service for footplate duties.

Chapter II
CHARIOT OF FIRE

It was February 1940, when my dream started to come true and I knocked on the office door of the Shed Boss. Wearing his bowler hat—it was almost a uniform in those days—the Shed Boss asked questions of the youthful aspirant stood in front of him. Many of those questions were important for determining character and suitability. Despite the quaking in my shoes, the answers must have proved to be satisfactory.

My height was measured and the details recorded on my application form; the standard height was around 5ft 6ins. Then came the extremely important test of the condition of my eyesight. Freedom from accidents and the safety of the passengers are paramount and naturally depend upon the good vision of the footplate men. Whether driving a main line express or yard shunter the men in the cab must instantly recognise and discriminate between various signals; defective vision must of necessity disqualify an otherwise competent man. Long after the ordeal of that first examination has been forgotten, periodic tests are applied at various stages of promotion and service.

I was tested in both eyes, and also in each eye separately, by means of a simple card test. Different colours, in squared and dotted formations, were required to be identified, counted, and other symbols distinguished from among them. The correctness and ease or otherwise of my answers were noted for possible future reference.

I signed the application form, and three days later I was officially informed that I had proved to be a successful candidate for foot-plate service.

Excitedly I reported for duty and was assigned my first employment in the yard. If I had thought that my work at the Mill was arduous, then, compared to the grind in that railway yard I didn't know I was born. But there was one important difference—here, I was doing what I wanted. That's not strictly true, of course, since I had higher ideals than shovelling coal, but I knew it was necessary if ever I was to hold the regulator in my hand.

Shovelling coal was literally my first job on the railway. Along with other lads, I had to empty coal wagons, and then stack the coal in readiness for the engines. It was extremely hard work, but like the rest, I attacked the job with enthusiasm.

Some days I would be detailed to tend the frost fires situated near to the water columns. A simple expedient to keep the water free of ice, but it also brought me closer to the locomotives. I would climb into the cab, and while the fireman busied himself with other aspects of his job, I was allowed to put coal on the fire. On others, I was put on a gang whose work was cleaning the engines as they 'came off' the line. Clad in cumbersome oilskins and wielding a thick black rubber hose, I had to wash the inside and outside of the locomotive. Thoroughness in this job is an absolute must. Other members of the gang wiped down and completed the engine's daily toilet.

The long and weary, but never dull, days had their reward when I was promoted to the post of packer. Now I could, at long last, really work on the engines—the other duties of course, had been work, but this job first began to give me the feel of the engine. I had to thoroughly overhaul all the working parts of both goods and passenger engines which were 'off duty'.

Inserting packing valves and joints during this virtual probationary period of my employment made me conversant with many different types and classes of locomotive. I was to gain much practical experience of these working parts which proved invaluable later on.

Of course, I was not alone on these jobs. While one of us on a particular team was working on the smoke-box, another would be in the cab or lying between the wheels. And always there was the vigilant, all-seeing presence of the foreman. Woe betide anyone whose work was below standard. He was not really a bad old stick, but sometimes the memory of him is so clear I can almost feel him breathing down my neck as he peered over my shoulder and pointed out something that was not quite right. Fortunately, that was not very often.

Finally, the day dawned when I was told that I would be examined by a footplate inspector for possible duties as a cleaner-fireman. I underwent another eyesight test, this time much more exhaustive. The test itself was an adaption of one used by Governmemt departments, particularly the Board of Trade when examining marine officers. I cannot remember the details of the numerous tests using spectroscopes and other sophisticated devices, but the memory of one of the card tests has remained with me. It involved the matching of numbered shades of colour on a card held by myself against those un-numbered on a card held by the examiner. Only he could see the matching list of numbers and shades, and he gave no sign as to whether or not I was correct.

As one may readily understand, the importance of good colour vision was, and still is, held in high regard by the railway authorities. Reds and greens have always been the leaf, flower, and fruit on the railway tree. To a person suffering from the commonest colour-blindness, the inability to distinguish between red and green, there is invariably one shade of green indistinguishable from white. Those who are unfortunate to be green-blind are characteristically confused by purples, grey, and bluish-green shades.

Scientifically selected confusion-colours were used at my examination, the object of the test being to determine my chromatic ability and thereby to detect any possible defects. As with all examinations of this nature, there is always someone helpfully ready with possible answers, and my experience proved to be no different in this respect. But no matter how carefully a candidate may have been primed in the art of matching the colours by their apparent density, the inevitable mistakes and obvious guesses betray the faulty vision. A modern analogy is to say that the test is rather like attempting to match colours on a black-and-white television set.

But for me, the examination held no problems, and I sailed through it. Similarly, I passed the oral part of the test and was now eligible for firing duties on the shunting engines.

My first firing job was an old saddle tank of the former Lancashire & Yorkshire Railway, shunting in the yards at Farington. As you may well imagine, space is at a premium on the footplate of these diminutive but extremely powerful locomotives. The proverbial cat would have had a hard time being there, I'll tell you. Eager and enthusiastic, trying to show how desperately keen I was for the job, the knuckles of my left hand took one hell of a battering from the hand-brake every time I swung the shovel. Until I got the swing of it, I reckon I put more coal on the footplate than in the fire-hole. The driver didn't take too kindly to this practice, and amongst the torrent of abuse which poured over my bowed head I think I heard the words "Clumsy Clot", or something to that effect. But as the days passed into weeks I grew in stature and regard from the driver. I was now able to fire the loco without littering his footplate.

The yards at Farington are on either side of the main London to Glasgow lines, and at various times between and during my duties I would watch the expresses thundering by. To the wonderful sound of their drum-beating motion as they flashed by in a spiral of smoke draped along the carriage roofs, I would conjure up my dreams. One day it would be my turn to be in command on one of those expresses.

I well remember some of those firemen as they went by. My presence on the little shunting engine was acknowledged in a salute later adapted by Winston Churchill as a Victory sign; in more recent times the salute received notoriety when practiced by an international show-jumper. It was a gesture of superiority, albeit accompanied by a grin. But my moment of revenge was near. It was to be the classic dream which was immortalised in the story, by Rudyard Kipling, of the shunting engine .007 rescuing the mighty Mogul locomotive, only this was for real.

On the 10th March, 1940, I was on the afternoon shift as the Midday Scot, on its way to Glasgow, ground to a halt at Farington Junction. The mighty 'Royal Scot' class locomotive had failed with injector trouble, and it was decided that our little shunt engine Number 11025 would perform the rescue operation. We would take the failed engine and its train into Preston station where another engine was to be provided.

I was so excited I could have jumped over the train, as I coupled our littl'un up to the giant 'Scot', watched by the driver and fireman. The latter made some crack about hoping I knew the difference between coupling links, hooks and eyes. The driver nodded, and said that he wondered if we knew the way to Preston. But my driver was an old hand at the game, and returned their 'come-uppance'. With a calm and serious voice, and an absolute 'dead-pan' face he said, "Oh yes, we are to shove you into the sidings at Preston, and leave you there to superintend the repairs. We'll work the train through to Carlisle.''

Away we went, trailing the two crewmen, the colour of whose faces matched the L.M.S. livery. We clanked along, down the bank, and in to Preston station. Novice that I was, up to that moment I really believed what my driver had said to the 'Scotties'.

Just picture the scene as we entered Number 5 Platform. A cheeky little shunting engine, snorting and sniffing with haughty disdain, trailing in its wake a red and shamefaced main-liner trying to hide in the sooty smoke. And the crew no doubt, wishing a hole would open in the track under us. But can you also imagine my feelings. The platform was on the fireman's side of the engine; I was as proud as the proverbial dog with two tails. I hung out of the cab side looking (or rather, trying to look) as if I'd brought the whole combination from Euston single-handed. As we came to a halt, the inevitable crowd gathered round us. Their faces were a picture. I wish I'd had a camera with me. Surprise, disbelief, shock, consternation, they were all registered on the sea of faces before me.

The station Chief Inspector instructed us to take the failed engine, the now humbled and once proud 'Scot', onto the Preston sheds.

''Yes sir,'' said the driver, and then in a slightly louder voice for the benefit of the crowd, ''We'll take her on to the sheds, and then come back and work the train forward to Carlisle''.

The Inspector looked stern and hard down his nose at my mate. He never said a word, the look was sufficient. But the play was not lost on the bowler-hatted gentry lining the platform; they laughed and applauded.

Needless to say, after safely disposing of the 'Royal Scot' class locomotive as per instructions, we were dispatched post haste back to the yard at Farington. Our moment of glory was over, but it could never be taken from us. We were the envy of the yard. But we were soon back to the routine of shunting.

As the weeks rolled by and my experience grew, I began to realise the important role played by the fireman in an engine crew. What I didn't learn from experience I was able to glean from my rule-book. I read this little volume time and again, as if my life depended on it. In a way I suppose it did, because the reading and learning of the rules in that book were necessary preparation for my main line fireman's examination. Every spare moment would find me pouring over that, by now, grubby work of reference.

The first rule in the 'Working of Trains' section stated, in words to the effect, that both the engine driver and the fireman had to be with their engine prior to its starting, and had to satisfy themselves that the locomotive was in proper working order.

Apart from the more obvious things like water, coal and oil, there had to be a full complement of equipment. Dependent upon the type of engine and its associated duties, this equipment included a certain number of lamps and detonators, two red flags, a fire-bucket, together with such tools as ordered by the Superintendent, not forgetting of course, the shovel, rakes, and coal hammer.

It goes without saying that the rule about driver and fireman not leaving their engine unattended, unless absolutely necessary, did not really need to have been written. No self- respecting loco man would leave his engine so that others could interfere with it. Other boots on the footplate? Not likely! It would be sacrilege.

As fireman, it was one of my principal duties to ensure that the coal on the tender was not stacked too high. A nasty avalanche could be caused if the engine stopped suddenly and large lumps of coal came cascading onto the footplate. But I had already learned my lesson about littering the footplate, a painful piece of education I wasn't anxious to repeat. What held good for the coal also held good for the equipment. The various boxes, fire-irons, and tools which are carried on the tender, need to be so placed that they are secured from falling off when the engine is in motion.

There is one rule, in various forms, which occurs in most of the rule books I have ever read. At first sight it looks to be a bit if a giggle, but in fact is a most serious rule. It reads—"The Engine-driver and Fireman must frequently during the journey look back to see that the whole of the train is following in a safe and proper manner". It would not improve the Company image for the Station Announcer to say that the next train to arrive at Platform 1 will be . . . and for a locomotive to come steaming along the ramp followed by a train of empty air! I'm kidding, of course, because a driver would feel the loss of his train, without needing to observe that it was no longer there. But the rule really hinges on the 'safe and proper manner' clause.

Eventually the day dawned for my examination which, hopefully, would qualify me for main line firing duties. By this time I was in a thorough state of readiness, my preparation being a long grind of painstaking study. I was confident, yet a little nervous, probably due to excitement.

I was instructed to report to the Footplate Inspector at Preston Station, a Mr. Harry Lloyd from Southport. My test was to be taken on the 1.18 pm Preston—Southport passenger train.

Any qualms I may have had about the firing part of my test soon disappeared as I stood before the firebox ready to rake and shoot the coal. I had always shown a willingness to fire on any engine, knowing that ultimately the experience would stand me in good stead. I was in my element, and my actions were second nature.

I passed the examination on all counts with flying colours, and shortly received notification that I was eligible to fire on main line locomotives. I felt justfiably satisfied. My promotion from cleaner to passed cleaner was a source of much delight to my parents. But long before then they had realised that I was that very rare and fortunate worker—a square peg in a square hole. The brash confidence of my boyhood and my subsequent persuasion of them had been justified.

My first duty after my promotion was on a night shift. As I walked to the sheds to report for duty, I had visions of mighty expresses thundering through the night, crossing the Blea Moor en route for Carlisle—the Night Mail must get through! Such were my fantasies about the job and how I would do it. As any other youngster with enthusiasm for his job, I planned and schemed, but without any real idea of what was actually required. As usual, my dreams and schemes were destined to be shattered, or at least, put in their proper perspective.

I reported for duty, and the foreman gave me my time card. He informed me that my job would be on the Preston pilot; this was a shunt engine of the Lancashire & Yorkshire saddle tank class 2 type which worked the Preston/East Lancs marshalling yards. A shunting engine—so much for the Night Mail to Carlisle!

The bitter pill of the foreman's orders brought me down to earth with a bump, somewhat deflating my ego in the process. It was going to be a long night, I could tell. However, my driver and I set forth for Preston.

Those of you who are familiar with the yard at Preston (East Lancs) will know something of what was likely to be entailed, and will appreciate the amount of work involved. Trains arrived at that busy yard, seemingly at every minute of the night and from every point of the compass. Apart from sorting out this 'tangle', there was also a gigantic warehouse to shunt. And if that was not enough, in between all these various duties my driver and I had to service our loco. Among other things, this included cleaning the fire, filling the tanks with water, and manually coaling the engine. For sheer hard graft manual coaling took some beating, especially at night, with all the extra hazards of wartime, not the least of which were the black-out regulations. The cleaning out of the fire kept my weight down and was not to my liking at all. I can recommend the method to modern devotees of the slimming cult, but ladies, be warned—the boiler suit is not the most glamourous of garments! With the black-out in operation, one had to be extremely careful at this cleaning job as a fireman it was my special duty to see that this work was carried out in a proper manner.

I raked the ashes and clinker, taking care not to disturb the bed of the fire, and poked them through a hole in the front end of the firebox, whence they fell into the ash-pan. My mate would be down below raking the hot ashes from the pan. At the instant they hit the ground my driver would throw a bucket of water over them to dispel the smouldering glow. Great clouds of stinking steam and sulphurous fumes came billowing up onto the footplate causing me to cough and splutter. As I near-on choked the driver saw in my discomfort a great source of amusement. Laughing with derision he taunted me with some caustic comment (which I certainly cannot repeat here), a remark to which, for once, I had no suitable reply.

About this time in 1941 the war was really being brought home to our erstwhile cosy little island; air-raids were becoming almost the order of the day. The wailing sirens gave warning of the approach of enemy bombers and well-rehearsed drills in factory and shop ensured that workers were safely sheltered by the time the raid occurred. But for the highly vulnerable trains with crew and passengers, such a system was impractical; in the open country there were no sirens, and in the towns and cities sirens were almost inaudible over the noise of the locomotive in steam. Clearly, a system had to be evolved which, if it could not afford protection, could at least give warning to the enginemen of impending air-raids.

The signalman was the person most in contact with the train crews, who literally looked to him for guidance. It was decided to use a colour-coded system which could also be operated orally. Coloured cards were displayed in the approach windows of the signal boxes. Purple for an impending air raid, red for enemy aircraft overhead, and green for all clear. According to the message they gave then appropriate action could be taken. The signalman, at his discretion and according to laid down rules, could stop the train and inform the driver at any time of the day.

I remember one day, we hitched up to a train of forty-five wagons laden with coal, and pulled out from Hoghton Station. As we approached the distant signal for Gregson Lane, which was in the Clear position, it suddenly whipped to Danger. Momentarily we were taken out of our stride, so to speak, by the abrupt change of signal. We were travelling on a falling gradient and fast approaching the signal, so you can imagine the frantic activity that was taking place on the footplate, especially when I tell you that we were riding a Class 7 freight engine with an 0-8-0 wheel arrangement.

I was swinging like a madman on to the hand brake, pouring with sweat, whilst my mate had the steam brake hard on. The motion was in reverse gear and was continually opening and shutting the regulator. And the distant signal was not now so distant! We were also sickeningly aware of another hazard, not yet visible—the crossing gates at Gregson Lane. As we approached, the track curved slightly to the right, and I was the first to see the home signal in the Stop position. I yelled out my news to my driver.

"How are the gates?", he yelled back at me.

"Closed to us", I replied.

With eyebrows raised, and a look of sublime acceptance, he coolly answered, "Well, lad, it'll not be long before they are open." He added, almost as an after-thought, "I reckon the station-master at Bamber Bridge will play merry hell with us if we arrive with crossing gates draped on the front of the loco."

What profound remarks may have been uttered by the station master, we shall never know. Our frantic efforts to stop proved successful and locomotive No. 9502 ground to a halt amid a shower of sparks at the foot of the signal post. The 'Bobby' (a railmans term of reference for a signalman),

Fowler 7F 0-8-0 No. 49664 was a fellow class member to 9502 (later B.R. No. 49502). This photograph catches 49664 in Wigan L. and Y. station sidings on 4th August, 1951. *(Norman Preedy)*

who had stood petrified at the top of the steps while our little drama unfolded before his popping eyes, came scurrying down. There was no need of words, neither comforting nor critical, as his breathless delivery of a message was comfort enough. He informed my driver that we were on Purple warning, then turned on his heel and hurried back to the signal box. The road was set, the crossing gates opened for us, and the signal lowered. With jets of steam snorting the wheels, slowly, cautiously, we began to move off.

We could feel the wheels beginning to bite at the rails, when the signalman dashed out of his box, and from the top of the steps yelled, "We're on Red." Barely had he uttered the words when there came a terrific bang. About a quarter of a mile ahead of us the scene erupted in an enormous explosion, and the shock waves shuddered along the track and through the train. A pall of black smoke hung over the confusion of the wreckage of a factory utterly demolished by high explosives. A disaster— yes; a tragedy—no. Fortunately it was Saturday afternoon, with only a skeleton staff on duty in the factory, none of whom were killed.

In this same year, another far more dramatic incident involving my colleagues at Lostock Hall took place. For them 1941 was a very significant page in their Book of Memories. Speeding the war effort meant, among other things, that regular runs were worked from the nearby munitions factory to Carlisle. The trains carrying this deadly cargo were routed via Blackburn and Hellifield. This stretch of line has some heavy gradients which could be very tricky to negotiate when hauling a heavy load.

One night, Driver Thompson and Fireman Wareing took their 0-8-0 locomotive to the factory sidings and backed onto their train. This particular one had a rake of some sixty vans containing a varied assortment of high explosives, bombs and shells—a frightening enough load at the best of times. The guard of the train was Mr. Pollard, also from the Lostock Hall stables. He went about his duties checking the train before reporting back to Driver 'Kicker' Thompson. ('Kicker' incidentally, had received his nickname many years previously for having planted four lace-holes of boot into an erring fireman who had chanced to upset him.)

The checking of a train according to the rule book can be a somewhat irksome chore, and most guards cut a few corners in the procedure. But an explosives train, especially in wartime, is not the best of articles with which to take liberties. Guard Pollard dutifully checked couplings, loadings, and brakes, wagon by wagon. The destination and warning labels were seen to be correctly placed and the lamps positioned according to the code. But this was a train with a difference, which needed extra precautions for the prevention of accident by fire or explosion. Under normal circumstances, not more than half a dozen wagons containing high explosives could be conveyed by any one train, and these had to be placed as far as practicable from the engine. This particular rake was ten times that amount.

The guard reported back to the driver, jokingly commenting that the springs on the vans were convex instead of being concave. Although in jest, the report conveyed the grim warning to the driver that he was about to haul an unusually heavy train. At 12.30 am precisely, they started their long and frighteningly eventful journey to Carlisle.

The short run to Lostock Hall Junction was perfectly ordinary, achieved without incident. They stopped at the Junction to take on water, and eventually the Class 7 locomotive resumed its journey, Bamber Bridge quickly slipping into the black of the night. From the Bridge there is a hard pull, which had the sturdy freighter grunting up to the intermediate block signal at Hoghton Tower. The tracks then led into a down gradient with a sharp dip known as Hoghton Bottoms. If a driver was not careful enough while traversing this dip he would receive a terrific snatch from somewhere in the train. This usually resulted in the train actually breaking loose from the engine. An entry would had to be made in the Journal, and many drivers claimed that the subsequent inquiry by the Superintendent of the Line was worse than the accident. But 'Kicker' Thompson was an experienced driver, and apart from the guard's report, he had long since realised that this was some train he had behind him. He remarked as much to Dick Wareing as they successfully negotiated the dip.

On a job like this there is no let-up for the fireman who has to maintain a head of steam at the right pressure ready for the driver the instant he needs it. Dick Wareing was steadily building up the fire, thicker at the back, and trimmed clean of ashes. One eye on the gauge, and one eye on the fire; a few lumps here, and a sprinkle of dust there, while the driver opened the regulator and brought the cut-off steadily back. Powerful rhythmic coughing from the pistons echoed from the inky gloom of the cuttings and bellowed from the embankments as they pulled into Blackburn. More water was taken on, then with the sanders on they negotiated the tunnel that joints onto Blackburn Station. On past the platforms, and up the bank to Wilpshire. As Driver Thompson gained speed over the top, little did he know that the 'fun' was about to start.

He closed the regulator and started to ease gently on the brake to bring the train together, when suddenly he felt the train, all sixty wagons of it, surge into the locomotive. The force of several hundred tons on a down gradient is about as sympathetic as a herd of angry rhinoceroses on the rampage. Full brake pressure was applied, and within seconds, the driver realised that due to their acceleration down Whalley Bank, they were 'running away'.

Driver Thompson pressed still harder against the brake lever, as if by some superhuman effort he could raise the pressure beyond the 220 pounds per square inch already registered on the polished brass gauge. But the steam brake was at its limit, and both crewmen were horribly aware that their efforts were futile. As if they had not enough worry on their plate, they both knew that within seconds they would be running over Whalley Viaduct, some 70ft above the River Calder. Familiar with their track and all its restrictions, both Thompson and Wareing knew that this viaduct had a permanant speed restriction of 5 miles per hour. As they approached Lango their estimated speed was in excess of 60 miles per hour!

By now, streamers of wind-whipped flames trailed from the brake blocks instead of the normal sparks. The runaway train descended onto the viaduct and hit it with such a shattering impact that for years afterwards 'Kicker' and his fireman swore that the viaduct actually swung from side to side. They claimed that its vibrations were so violent at the fury of their onslaught that they could see, as well as feel, its superstructure move.

Eventually, perhaps as much with 'Divine' intervention as the combined skills of Messrs. Thompson and Wareing, the wayward locomotive was brought safely under control. The rest of the journey was an anti-climax for the two sweat soaked railmen.

After the filing of their report the Inspector of the Line closed the section for two whole days while teams of construction engineers examined the entire viaduct and its supports. At the ensuing inquiry the times entered in various logs (which are made for all trains to account for their journeys) showed that the recorded time of the train's arrival at Low Moor Crossing proved its speed to have been 80 miles per hour as it crossed the viaduct!

In contrast to this rather harrowing tale, an experiance I am glad I did not have to endure, there is the rather apocryphal story which I am sure could have been heard in any steam-engine shed. It concerns the young passed cleaner on his first firing job. The engine was blowing like mad, the entire loco wreathed in a cloud of white steam. The driver turned to his mate and said,

"Crikey! We are in good nick aren't we?"

"Aye! we are that. We've plenty of steam and two boilers full of water", the young lad replied.

"Two boilers full of water?", echoed the driver, unable to believe his ears.

In a broad Lancashire accent the lad replied, "Aye. One at my side and one at yours", pointing proudly at the two boiler gauge glasses.

What the driver said does not appear to have been recorded. I'll bet he could have matched his engine for steam pressure.

But the story does call to mind a gospel-true tale of a young fireman, whose identity I will hide under the name of 'Fred', who worked in the Preston area. One night, his train was rolled into Preston station, sorted, carded, and coupled into two portions, one for Manchester and one for Liverpool. The shunter divided the train, after which, the young fireman coupled his locomotive to the Liverpool portion. The guard came along the train, inspecting the coaches, and reported to the driver, giving him the composition (number of coaches, weight, etc.). The young lad heard him refer to ten coaches. This he decided was too much, so he jumped off the footplate while the driver and guard conferred and went to the fifth coach, uncoupling it from the other half of the train. He climbed back on board the engine, checked the fore, and waited for the guard's signal to his driver to roll 'em. The signal was received and away they went, leaving half of the train standing at the platform, and the guard shouting and waving frantically into the unresponsive wraiths of steam and smoke which drifted by.

As they pulled away from Number 6 platform the driver said,

"This is a light train we're pulling tonight, Fred. What have we got—a wagon load of feathers?"

Proud as a peacock, fireman Fred replied, "Aye, it is that. It should be, an' all. I uncoupled five, I thought ten coaches were too many for us on a night like it is, an' all."

It would have needed a very strong-willed man not to have made some succinct and pithy comment in reply. Perhaps it is as well that the sound of the locomotive hid the remarks of the driver from the ears of any innocent bystanders.

Chapter III
FOOTPLATE TURNS.

Just before the end of the war in 1945, I climbed another rung in my ladder of ambition. I was made a regular fireman on the passenger train services running between Preston, Blackpool, Southport, Todmorden and through to Manchester Victoria.

The locomotive stock at that time was mainly Class 4 Tanks with 4-6-4 wheel arrangement. In the opinion of most of the drivers and firemen, myself included, these were a very good and efficient engine; they had the extra advantage of being quite comfortable to work on. However on occasions the work load would be very great, and because of duty and maintenance rosters, the number of locomotives of this class available would be small, so another class would be used. These were the notorious Lancashire & Yorkshire Class 3F 0-6-0's. Believe me, these engines were, to say the very least, a different kettle of fish. A brief account of these two Classes will give you a closer insight to my reactions on the footplate.

It was late in 1889 when the first of a new design by J. A. F. Aspinall appeared on the tracks, sturdy 6-wheelers which could knock up a good turn of speed. The improved boiler heating surface area of just over 1200 sq.ft. was achieved despite the restrictions of a shorter boiler than the 2-4-2 Tanks which had only just preceded this new class. The working pressure was rated at 160psi.

During the next twelve years 400 of these new locomotives were built, with a few variations over the years in the dimensions of the cylinders. The size of the tender was somewhat on the small side with a water capacity of 1800 gallons and 3 tons of coal. The coal area was below the footplate level, and with the firebox about two feet above the firing of these *****! was quite a feat of balance and skill.

From the completion of the class to just prior to the grouping of the railways, nearly one hundred were rebuilt. Some were fitted with unsuperheated Belpaire boilers, which improved the ratio of water and steam in the boiler; some had Hughe's Belpaire boilers with Schmidt superheaters, while others had Hughe's superheaters. Although better suited to the hauling of passenger trains, the Class 3 0-6-0's were frequently to be seen hauled heavy goods trains.

With the formation of the London, Midland & Scottish Railway in 1923, the class were re-distributed throughout the new Company's network. Some historians have taken their sturdiness and simple design as evidence of popularity, especially as they were much pressed into service during the summer for the hauling of special trains. But while this may have been true at the turn of the century, certainly no driver or fireman with whom I had contact had a good word to say for them. For all practical purposes the cab

Ex Lancashire & Yorkshire class 3 0-6-0 No. 52515 saw service into 1963, latterly as works shunter at Horwich. The hated cut-out cab side can be seen in this study taken at Horwich. (*M. Taylor*)

was virtually non-existent—we used to reckon that the canopy was hardly deep enough to cover the gauges, let alone the footplate crew. The curved cut-out cab sides were murderous wind collectors, and with the inclement weather for which the British Isles, and the Manchester area in particular, is famous, drivers and firemen on the almost totally exposed footplate certainly earned their coppers. A fireman would seem to spend his entire working day bringing coal forward on the tender or cleaning the fire, and, without respite from the other two jobs, taking on water; they were very thirsty locos.

Lest it seem that I am complaining too much about a product of a much-revered designer, let me hasten to add that I can say one good thing about these monstrosities for which Lostock Hall was noted. They had a good whistle, vibrant and melodic. But here's the rub—quite often it was not possible to raise enough steam to blow it!

The 4-6-4 Tanks were built as replacements for locomotives operating in suburban areas, mostly 4-6-0 tanks. They first appeared in service early in 1924, and with their extended front framing and larger bogies were at the time the largest British-built tank engines. In contrast to the deadly Class 3F, these locomotives were luxury indeed, having a canopy which was integral with the bunker. With two fairly large windows on each side of the cab, and a nine foot footplate, it was almost like home from home. The weight was fairly evenly distributed, making for a nicely balanced engine which was comfortable to work.

There's no pleasing some folks, and the critics of these Class 4's were no exception. Despite their popularity with the crews and its superb power, they were picked to pieces by the 'boffins', and finally Stanier scrapped the class altogether. This was a great pity for surely such a handsome and efficient engine deserved a better fate? I am pleased that I had the experience of working one of the few which survived the combined destructive efforts of the CME and the war.

One day, soon after becoming a regular fireman, I was booked on duty, wondering what the day's job would be, when the foreman called me over to his desk.

"How would you like a fresh job today, Bert? I am one fireman short for the 2.20 am Bamber Bridge to Wakefield run. How about it?"

Like any footplate-man, I was always on the look-out for extra cash in my pay-packet. I weighed up the situation like lightening, wondering why the foreman was grinning.

"Certainly gaffer, anything you say."

Then he dropped the bombshell in my shovel, so to speak.

"The driver is waiting for you across the yard. The engine number is 12101."

He couldn't have floored me more effectively if he had hit me with a shovel. I closed my eyes and positively wilted. Why couldn't I keep my big mouth shut? 12101 was one of the dreaded 3F's!

My driver and I soon got her trundling out of the yard, but she made hard work of it. Perhaps the lead in my boots and the sag in my shoulders as I slouched across the yard had rubbed off on her. We steamed away with a load of forty-five empty coal wagons and just managed to roll into Hoghton station, just four miles from our starting place. There was no water in the boiler and a mere eighty pounds of steam showing the glass.

We stopped outside the signal box and the signalman opened a window to enquire of the driver the reason for this unscheduled stop.

My mate called up. "We'll have to wait for about ten minutes while we raise some steam in this old tin can."

"Very good", replied the 'bobby', "I have the kettle on the boil if you want any tea."

As quick as a flash, my mate retorted "Yes please. I'll bet there's more steam in your kettle than in our engine. Pour it in the top."

We swigged at the welcome tea, and eventually, with ourselves and the engine having recovered strength, we continued on our journey with a full head of steam, and hopefully, with a boiler full of water.

At this stage I decided to clean the tube plate. This was a joint operation which first of all meant emptying the sand-box which was situated under the fireman's side of he footplate, and filling the shovel with sand. My mate got the engine working heavily up a gradient, and then kicked open the firebox door. In went the shovelful of sand which I placed on the face of the tube plate.

If any of today's conservationists and anti-pollutionists had been around at the time, questions would have been asked in Parliament. And if the Railway Inspector had been on the spot I would have been for the 'high jump'. The company rules quite clearly stated that engine-drivers and firemen "must so arrange their fires as to avoid any unnecessary emission of smoke from their engines". The result of my little sanding operation was an instant black-out of the surrounding countryside. Palls of sooty smoke hung around for ages, but it had a marvellous effect on the steaming capability of the locomotive.

For a relatively short time I worked my duty on a score of different engines, each with different drivers. It was not until I teamed up with Tom Barlow that my career once more began to assume direction. He was my first regular driver on the passenger trains, and I could not have wished for a more likeable, easy-going work-mate than Tom. He was a brilliant engineman who really knew his engine and every sleeper-end wherever he travelled. In point of fact, it used to be said that he knew the roads so well that the signals would nod at him when he passed them by. Such acord from among the ranks of footplatemen is praise indeed.

It used to be a marvel for me to watch him at work in wintertime; I realise now that what he did was one big 'show-off', especially for my benefit. What was, strictly speaking, unsafe working, would not have been attempted had not Tom got prior knowledge of the circumstances, of which I knew little or nothing.

His favourite trick was to stand with his back to the partly open door of the firebox—"Warming my brains", he used to say—watching the countryside fly past over the top of the footplate doors. He knew the instant we were approaching a set of signals merely by reading the landmarks. As the footplate swayed beneath him, he would take up the rhythm, sway over onto his right leg, peer out along the track at the signal and note its position. If it was in the clear, he would resume his stance; if however, the signal was at caution he would swing round to the controls, looking as if he had never left them, ready for any emergency. None ever arose, but it was on these occasions that the parentage of the signal man came in for some ripe criticism because the said gentleman had disturbed Tom from a warm and comfortable place.

I felt a great deal of respect and warm admiration for Tom, both as a driver and as a man. Nothing ever seemed to upset his equanimity. If the engine was running well there was no cause for bother, and if its working were less than perfect and not up to Barlow standards, then he applied his pet formula to the restoration of perfection. He would view the situation with an almost blithe tranquillity and then turn to me and say, "Never mind Bert, there's a nice little signal box ahead. We will have ten minutes to get some steam up (or whatever needed attention), and while you attend to that I'll go and make the tea."

This always sounded like a good idea to me. It still does. It's quite a surprise how many of life's problems can be resolved by a quiet contemplation over a 'cuppa'.

Many thanks, Tom, for all you did for me. Also to the many others of the Lostock Hall sheds who unstintingly gave me the benefit of their knowledge and experience. Their precious gift was to stand me in good stead in later years.

It was another driver, the late Jack Gabbott, who first let me drive a train. Although he is no longer with us, he will always be one of my heroes of the footplate, a first-class man and driver. I had been with him for some time, but he didn't have much to say, indeed I sometimes used to wonder if he even knew I was there. One day, quite out of the blue, he turned to me and said, "Bert, I've been watching you for some time as you've done your job."

Wasn't he satisfied with my firing? I thought I was alright. Was I going to get reported to the Shed Boss for bad workmanship? Surely not. His next words so astounded me that I could not speak—I could only gape and splutter.

"I've been thinking. It is high time that you started to learn the job on this side of the footplate." If my mouth had been a tunnel he could have driven the train in!

Now my firing duties began to take on a new dimension. With each shift I would make up the fire and raise the steam, and under Jack's guidance I would proudly sit in the driver's seat. Nature's elementals, fire and water, began to have a new significance for me. I began to understand why it was important for the driver to have steam at his command instantly, why he wanted it when he wanted it.

Jack would stand behind me showing the stretches of track where the regulator needed to be open, or could be closed, where the brakes needed application and how much, and where an engine would run without steam. He taught me the gradients and how to feel them, how to make the locomotive respond accordingly. I learned where to look for the different signals, and how to react. All priceless lessons which I have never forgotten.

I knew beforehand of the peculiarities of different locomotives but I never really understood the whys and wherefores. Take two engines from the sheds, give them the same treatment from first firing to cleaning out the firebox, and you'll have problems. One engine will be perfect in every way, even though you treat her casually, firing when you think about it. The other engine will have you struggling all day, needing to be fired very lightly and very often. I was once told that locomotives are like ladies, they have to be wooed and won before they will respond. There are a thousand and one reasons why this should be so and it would take a lifetime of experience and skill to explain why. With Jack behind me I learned their wiles and picked up a few of my own to combat these temperamental rogues on wheels.

These early driving lessons, I am happy to say, continued each day for several months, and after a while I never used to think about it very much, fondly imagining that once clear of the yard (also including the Shed Boss) we were in a little world of our own. So long as the job was done properly and no unusual reports requiring investigation came back down the line everything was alright. It therefore came as quite a surprise when the Shed Boss sent for me, and as I stood by his desk he told me that he had been getting good reports about me and my driving. He said that he thought the time had come when by virtue of my seniority and knowledge I should be taking my test for driving. I could scarcely refrain from adding, ''I've been thinking that for years.'' Me a passed fireman. It was the very thing I had been working for since that very first day way back in 1940.

And so fifteen years after I had knocked on the office door of the Shed Boss I climbed yet another rung in the ladder of my ambition. On March 16th, 1955, I took the first part of my driving test, a full eight hours of questions and answers about rules and regulations. I thought I knew them all, but by golly, some of those questions really had me digging deep; half-way through I was prepared to believe that the examiner had thrown another Company's Rule Book into the pot for good measure.

But I survived the day, and the following one, which was an eight hour stint of putting into practice what I had been 'doing' in the book of words. This, for me, was the real test,—driving. I had to pass this one to be able to live with myself, especially after the fuss and bother I had caused with my Mum and Dad.

The tension which builds up in a person prior to these examinations is quite tremendous, probably something akin to 'stage fright' in an experienced actor. Literally, one is on trial, and all those things one has reckoned to know, suddenly have to be proved to an impartial examiner. One's career is in the balance so the simple human frailty of nervousness is not unexpected.

For my part, I have always upheld the notion that rules are for the guidance of wise men and the observance of fools. Whenever necessary or possible I have bent the rules as the circumstances dictated—but always I observed the spirit of those rules. Although I avow their absolute necessity for the safety of the passengers, train crew, and Company alike, I always found their learning to be a most boring and irksome task.

But now I was to be tested to see how well I had read the little forenote prior to Page 1 in the Rule Book—

''Every Servant supplied with this Book must make himself thoroughly acquainted with, and will be held responsible for a knowledge of, and compliance with, the whole of the following Rules and Regulations, and any modifications thereof made as above mentioned.''

Chapter IV
IN THE SEAT OF THE MIGHTY.

I took my driving test in Southport, or rather from Southport. The part of my test which actually took place in that town was concerned with my mechanical knowledge of the glorious beast. Apart from watching the line he is travelling and judging his speed to a nicety, the steam-engine driver needs to listen to every beat of the engine, and instantly to perceive and be able to diagnose the most minute irregularity. Above all, he must be prepared to tackle any necessary remedial work to get the locomotive back to its depot. I had read of some drivers uncoupling one set of wheels, thereby making the cylinders drive on one side only, in the event of a side-rod breaking.

I thought of all this sort of thing as I walked through the streets of Southport to the sheds where I had to prepare a locomotive for the road. To do this I had to start literally at the beginning by reading the notice board to see if my engine had been given clearance from the sheds, and then going over to the stores to collect the necessary lamps and oil for the journey. I was required by the examiner to oil the motion and bogies and check the brakes, the latter being one of the most important duties a driver must perform before setting out. This was all done to the examiner's apparent satisfaction, then he asked me to make some trimmings.

I looked at him as if I hadn't heard him right, but I had; my heart sank. I knew what he meant alright because I'd watched a few drivers making them. Trimmings are the loco man's term for a contrivance made of wire and having a worsted tail. They are hung in the oil boxes and syphon oil along the worsted to the various points requiring lubrication. But watching was all I had done, I had never made a trimming in my life.

It is quite a work of art to make a good trimming, and some of those drivers I used to watch were real experts at the job. Their manual dexterity was such that I used to think it not too much of an exaggeration to reckon that they could have taken a job any day as a watchmaker or a magician. On this day in Southport my fingers were all thumbs, and at this, my first attempt, I made a right hash of the job.

The inspector took one look at my handiwork, and with his long-suffering eyes raised heavenwards, he caustically said, "It looks more like a rat's tail than a trimming."

Fortunately for me, he took a lenient view of the situation and said that he thought it would be to my advantage if I were to spend a little time practising making trimmings a bit better. Actually, I never made another from that day to the day when I regretfully and prematurely left my employment in the railways.

The footplate inspector's lot, like Gilbert's policeman, is not a happy one. Certainly on examination days there can be few people who like him;

careers can be made or broken on the strength of his report. To the biased view of the examinee the inspectors seem so very cocksure; they know all the answers, and they represent authority. With the tolerant view of twenty years hindsight I can appreciate that they are merely displaying the very human trait of showing just how much they do know. After all, their questions and the manner of their asking becomes so repetitious that the whole ritual must be burned into their very souls. Such day in, day out custom must mean that they know their rules and regulations backwards and their locomotives inside out.

Like every other trade and profession, the ranks of the footplate inspectors have their good 'uns and their bad 'uns. I once knew a footplate inspector who made tape recordings of himself reading questions and answers from the rule book and law manuals relating to the Carriers' Act. Everything had to be done according to the rule, he was inflexible. But I must hasten to add that not all footplate inspectors are of this calibre; although I took a somewhat jaundiced view of my particular inspector on examination day, I realise that he was one of the good 'uns. He must have been—he passed me!

I was successful on the first day's examination of my knowledge of the rules an regulations, and on the second day I renewed my acquaintance with the inspector to take my practical driving test. The 1.18 pm from Preston to Southport was an historic train, if not in British Railways annals

Resting at Carlisle Kingmoor shed on 16th June, 1963 is Fowler 2-6-4T No. 42301, which belonged to the same class as (4) 2434. *(Norman Preedy)*

then certainly in mine. I am sure that Class 4 Tank No. 2434 never had a more determined driver; I wish that she were still around now.

These Class 4 Tank loco's had an unfortunate peculiarity about which I was warned before I set off. Usually when stopping, the boiler injector would knock off with a deafening roar of steam. This blasted out from the waste water pipe which was slung from just under the bottom step leading to the footplate. This could be very dangerous indeed for anyone who had the misfortune to be standing in the vicinity. Many a ganger or trapper has had to receive hospital treatment for scalded legs caused by these engines. People, especially those visiting the various preserved railway sites throughout the country, do not seem to appreciate that the steam from a locomotive is considerably hotter and more concentrated than that from a kettle—and that can give you a nasty burn.

But back to that day in Preston. To counter this tendency to blow-off, I was shown how to hold the steam brake in position as the vacuum brake was applied to the train. I took the lesson to heart, the procedure had the desired effect, and consequently I had a trouble free journey to Southport.

The ordeal of my second day of examination ended with my inspector passing me as a driver—but not before he had imparted a few choice words of wisdom. He properly deflated my ego and let it be clearly known that my first job as a driver would not be as the man in charge of the Royal train.

Then he said, "Watch the rule book, Mr. Stewart. Keep out of trouble and keep your nose clean, which translated means 'Out of trouble, out of mind'." His final words of warning I heeded throughout my driving career. "Stop on the correct side of the 'Stop' signals. If you go by a 'Stop' signal, you will find yourself on the carpet with your cap in your hand quicker than you can say 'Home and distant'."

At last I was qualified to sit in the seat of the mighty. Those wonderful dreams from the days of Bradshaw Field were about to be realised as dreams come true.

As a passed fireman I was eligible to drive any kind of train, and since I was now one of the elite, my pay-packet would be enriched accordingly. All I now wanted was sufficient driving turns to acquire my enhanced pay. Rather less than befits the mighty this was the magnificent sum of one shilling per driving turn on top of my fireman's rate of pay. In order to qualify for this shilling I had to operate a minimum stint of two hours driving.

There must have been a million ways for passed firemen to achieve this desirable end. Driving turns to a young passed fireman were absolutely vital, indeed essential, if he was to achieve his ultimate goal. In those days 365 turns qualified a man to receive a rise in pay as a first year driver. Progression occurred until the maximun turns were being worked and then the man got the rate which qualified him in status and duties as a Full Driver.

It used to be said that a passed fireman would do anything, even contemplate murder (Shed Bosses and Drivers beware), to get himself a driving turn. This was not strictly true, being a fallacious comment upon the firemens' zeal, but I can assure you that the competition was extremely keen. The way some of those chaps used to fill in their route cards, one could be forgiven for thinking that the railway lines were made of elastic!

If a passed fireman went sixty miles from his depot and marked the same on his route card, the next fireman to travel the same route would do his darndest to make the journey register as sixty-five miles. This increased his chances over the first fellow for qualifying for the coveted status. It was the proverbial rat race, with the law of the jungle brought to the railway tracks. Many hot and harsh words were spoken in the mess rooms about the ethics of various practices employed to acquire driving turns.

I suppose that I was as guilty as the next man in trying to achieve my ambition ahead of the others. Ahead, yes; at the expense of, no. On reflection, I can honestly say that I did not do badly in achieving maximum driving turns, and my goal was reached without the use of malicious practice.

The system was more at fault than any of the men. I took three and a half years to arrive at my maximum; I had a very good route card which covered some one thousand track miles. But such a route card does not mean that I journeyed one thousand miles from my depot—the figure includes the return journey. For instance, a journey to Blackpool, twenty-five miles from the depot, would make a round trip of fifty miles to be entered on the route card. It has been argued that the return journey should not be included on a driver's record since he has to return to the depot anyway. But he has to drive those track miles back and so his route card should stand as a factual record of accomplishment.

For reasons best known to themselves, I suppose, some drivers were not interested in furthering their experience. For them, their vision extended no further than the buffer beams at the end of the yard. These drivers and passed firemen would not even consider taking main line driving turns. They were just content to knock wagons about in the marshalling yard or do passenger shunting in the stations where necessary. One cannot blame them if they were contented with such a situation—after all, in the stress and strain of modern living, job contentment is a much envied prize. Or perhaps they knew their own limitations, an equally enviable state. As far as I was concerned I wanted no part of this state of affairs, except perhaps where shunting occurred in my normal turn of duty. But even then I would look for a chap with whom I could swap. Sometimes I was successful and sometimes I wasn't. On these latter occasions, fortunately few in number, I would handle the regulator reluctantly—me of all people, who had wanted so much to be an engine-driver. My eyes would be cast in envious glances at the main line flyers going by on the tracks at the far side of the yard.

But looking back, it was all experience of one sort or another. The footplate has always proved to be a good source of both technical know-how and good-natured banter. One incident illustrating this latter aspect of the 'Brotherhood of the Footplate' occurred on one of my shunting teams.

I had worked my little shunter to the north end of Platform 5 at Preston Station and had her standing there, simmering gently. The telegraph bell rang and the station announcer gave details of the incoming London to Glasgow express. In she steamed, headed by a magnificent 'Duchess', and pulled alongside and stopped with her footplate opposite ours. The driver, a Camden man, looked down at us and with a broad Cockney accent, and grin to take the sting out of his words, said, "Whatch'er cock. Do you get paid for working on those egg-boilers?"

My mate was equal to the occasion, always being ready with a quick retort, and referring to the driver's big nose, told him to mind it. "If you stick it over the side when you leave here mate, you'll bring all the telegraph poles down." Although neither of us could know it at the time, the Cockney driver and myself were to meet later on.

Another incident, while not qualifying for the technical know-how category, certainly comes into the 'Things I'll not do twice' section of footplate experience. I once did firing duty for a driver who was one of the good old school. He was extremely conscientious and meticulous; everything had to be done absolutely dead right for his satisfaction. And he checked. But for once, on this occasion, he failed to.

I remember we worked an empty stock train from Lostock Hall to Euxton R.O.F. to take the workers home to Manchester. The headlight code at the time required an empty train to exhibit a lamp on the top bracket and one on the right-hand buffer bracket, and as part of my fireman duties I had to attend to the important matter. On my arsival at Euxton I was supposed to alter the lamp code, putting a lamp on either buffer bracket thereby showing the train to be an 'Express Passenger'. For some reason unknown, we both had a lapse of memory. I forgot all about altering the lamps, and my stickler-for-detail mate forgot to check. The platform whistle blew, to be answered by a hoot from us, and amid great clouds of hissing steam, locomotive Class 4 Tank No. 2434 departed the station.

My driver suddenly exclaimed, "Did you remember to alter the lights laddie?"

"Good heavens, no," I said, "I didn't".

His face didn't alter by one wrinkle. He continued to look ahead, his face resolute and determined, his hand firmly on the controls. In a calm, matter-of-fact voice, he said, "Well, they will have to be altered before we pass the next signal box—and I'm not going to stop the train."

I looked at him a bit open mouthed. "How the heck do you think I'm going to alter them if you don't stop the train?"

His answer made me certain I was riding with a lunatic. "You'll have to climb through the front observation window and walk along to 'em."

I looked down at the 4-6-4 wheel arrangement grinding along the rails, and I thought to myself, "This chap has gone daft." However, it seemed that he was serious, so I opened the small window to be hit by what seemed like a Force 9 gale. I squeezed through the narrow aperture in a far from elegant posture. The British Olympic Gymnastic Team lost a star performer that night. I inched my way along the top of the tank side, clambered along to the front end and lifted the lamp from the top of the smoke box. My eyes glazed as I leaned over the buffer beams, the sleepers a blur as they disappeared beneath the thrashing wheels. I placed the lamp in the correct position on the other buffer bracket. Then I made my perilous way back.

On regaining the relative safety of the observation window I had the undignified performance to repeat in reverse. I entered head first and dropped on my hands onto the box a good two feet below the window level. Perhaps all this would have made a circus acrobat feel great, but it did nothing for me except to make me feel angry with myself, and humiliated into the bargain. The only response it evoked from the driver was, "Let that be a lesson to you." I said nothing, my jaws clamped tightly together. Needless to say, it was!

Chapter V
ON THE BOIL

During this period in my career a gradual, but welcome, change was taking place at Lostock Hall. At long last, the ex-LMS Class 5MT 4-6-0's, popularly known as 'Black Fives', were replacing the old L & Y Class 3's and the 'Austerities'.

In my early days as a fireman I had cursed the Class 3 six-wheelers, but I reckon that the War Department's grim looking 'Austerity' model would run them a very close second on my 'hate' list. Dull and dirty in their wartime livery, monstrous in their design, they evoked no charitable thoughts from the crews who were unfortunate enough to be detailed to work them. I honestly believe it to be no exaggeration to say—"I have never worked on a more awkward engine in my life than this type."

Nothing would respond to you, either as driver or fireman. Coaxing and cursing were equally useless with these hunks of machinery; they were as responsive as blocks of granite on wheels. The injector steam wheels were situated in the corner in front of the fireman; to turn these on was a battle of determination, resolved only by the use of persuasive methods, namely, the coal pick. The reason? At any speed in excess of 25mph, they locked in position when being turned off. This would trigger off a violent bucking reaction between the engine and the tender. You can imagine the effect that this had if one had a tender of small coal aboard! The sloping pile of nuts would begin to disintegrate and in a rattling cascade a black avalanche would quickly spread over the footplate, with a billowing cloud of coal dust enveloping the sweating crew, causing immense discomfort. The unfortunate fireman, staggering about on the unsteady plate, had his work cut out in a desperate endeavour to repel this invasion by the black gold. While tending the fire it meant that every other swing of the shovel had to be a throw back into the tender.

During the coal crisis of the Fifties the National Coal Board came up with some concoction dreamed up in their laboratories. The result looked like some rough, black eggs laid by pre-historic birds in a science fiction fantasy. The railways were obliged to use this substitute and it was a very common sight to see tenders brimming full of these egglets. The tremendous shaking which one experienced on the 'Austerities' caused the unstable load of egglets to flow almost knee deep. They were very brittle, and the dust, together with the chemical contents, would irritate the eyes and cause great distress. So much so, that the firemen continually had to receive treatment at the nearest hospital. This happened to me on several occasions, much to my discomfort.

The advent of the Class 5MT's made a tremendous difference to the depôt. We were getting a wider variety work, and these 'Black Fives' were masters of their task. They were justifiably regarded by crewmen and

'Black Five' 4-6-0 No. 45305 stands on Lostock Hall shed. (Norman Preedy)

enthusiasts alike as possibly the most successful multi-purpose engines on British Railways. They were first introduced in 1934 by Mr.W.A.Stanier, the Chief Mechanical Engineer of the London, Midland & Scottish Railway. Abandoning the building of the 2-6-0 'Mogul' type locomotive, Stanier quickly introduced these new two-cylinder 4-6-0's, intended for general purpose duties. Over the heavy gradients of the Midlands they proved to be ideal engines for the job. More than 840 were built, distinguishing themselves during wartime service, at least twelve have been saved from the scrapman's torch by loving preservationists.

These majestic locomotives, with a tender capacity of 4,000 gallons, were very light on water consumption. With a boiler pressure of 225lbs. per sq. inch pumping into 18½″ x 28″ cylinders and powering 6ft. diameter driving wheels, their exceedingly free steaming capabilities were fully and efficiently exploited. They were a fireman's dream, and to drive them was pure heaven. It did not matter what type of work they were called upon to do—fast heavy freights, slow coal hauling, long-distance express passenger or local stopping trains—they made beautifully light work of anything and everything that they did. A truly great engine and a credit to the chap who designed them.

At this time I was doing quite a lot of express work between Preston and Carlisle; the latter station could easily be the sole subject of a romantic history of British railways. From the earliest days of the Newcastle and

Carlisle Railway to the latter days of the LMS it has been a major junction. Prior to the 1923 re-grouping, when the London, Midland & Scottish became the sole proprietor of the station, no fewer than seven railway companies used its facilities under the management of the Carlisle Citadel Station Joint Committee. This Committee was accorded the status equivalent to that of a joint railway company, the station being in fact jointly owned by the Caledonian and the London & North Western Railways.

Our route to Carlisle lay via Blackburn, Hellifield and the rugged Blea Moor, and we would return the next day through Penrith, across Shap, and down to Carnforth. In the summertime, the run down from Hellifield never failed to inspire me. The down gradient is only a brief stretch of track, and the journey into Settle Junction is so swiftly made, that it is often momentarily difficult to realise that one's speed is in the region of seventy miles per hour. At the junction, where the railroads part company, one set of tracks sweep away to the left, carrying the Lancaster and Morecambe traffic, whilst we carried straight on up the bank towards Blea Moor. It was a glorious thrill in the early hours of the morning, just when the bright golden disc of the sun made dazzling shafts of light through the trees, to hear the mighty drumming beat of the engine as she worked at full stretch, reaching for the top of the bank in an almost human cry of exultation.

But as if all this were not enough, I was regaled by the sight of a first class fireman doing his job. While holding the regulator, feeling the pulse of the engine (almost like a part of me), keeping an eye on the track ahead, noticing the thousand and one things alongside and beyond the tracks, I still found time to watch him firing expertly and keeping the footplate clean and tidy. When the fire had been banked and trimmed sufficient to keep the needles steady in the gauges, he used the slaking pipe to damp down the coal dust, sweep away the thin black paste, and finish off by brushing up with a small hand brush. I swear that after these methodic efforts one could have confidently eaten a meal from off the footplate.

Many times on such a journey I have sung numerous operatic arias in harmony(?) with the fireman. While La Scala Teatro, Milan, would not have been hard pressed to find a Primo Tenore, and while I am certain that by no means could we have won any prizes for our duets, I am equally certain that we demonstrated the existence of a cordial bond. Alas! on every footplate this was not always the case, and dis-harmony filled the cab. I have known drivers and firemen not to speak to each other outside the line of duty, and then only at the barest minimum, for days on end. Fortunately, this was a rare occurrence, and the least said the better.

Reaching Blea Moor tunnel, the sanders were turned on to prevent the odds-on certainty of the wheels slipping inside the damp confines of the subway. These were kept on until about or beyond the halfway mark, when one could feel the surge of acceleration as the train hit the level stretch of track prior to Aisgill Summit. We thundered past the signal-box splitting the air with our trilling whistle, and with a thumbs up greeting to the signalman.

The curving track and viaduct in the shadow of Wild Boar Fell were a prelude to the Summit, but leaving Aisgill we started to fly down the bank past Mallerstang. The name is derived from the Welsh 'moel' or 'bare hill', and the Norse 'stong', or 'boundary'. This lonely but scenic valley is close to the Yorkshire border. The engine was now gently rolling, gradually picking up speed, then the needle registered 80mph and she was going "like a bomb". Two heads peered out from the cab sides, eyes squinting into the wind so as not to miss a signal, ears flattened back as the miniature gale whistled past. We grabbed a bacon sandwich and a lid of tea from the billy-can, watching the beautiful ever-changing magic of the countryside as it flashed by. Could anyone ask for more than perfect bliss?

We are riding on a unique stratch of British railway history here. The 73-mile length of the Settle & Carlisle Railway, later to become part of the Midland Railway, itself swallowed up by the mighty London, Midland & Scottish Railway, was hewn out of the barren, rocky wilds by navvies between 1869 and 1875. It is the highest stretch of railway line in England and also the most expansive line in Britain, laid at a cost (at the time) of £47,500 per mile.

As we flashed through Appleby, I opened the regulator once more, coaxing more power from the engine to get us up and over the short rise past Newbiggin. Then, as the drumming beat of the pistons grew stronger, vibrating through the entire frame, we roared by the Anydrite Quarry at Long Meg. The slashing blur of the sleepers and tracks disappeared into the needle point of infinity as we pounded through the ever beautiful Lazonby, with its red sandstone cutting, nearly 50 feet deep and a third of a mile long.

This beautiful, fertile Vale of Eden is indeed a paradise, especially for those who pursue the endeavours of Izaac Walton, the celebrated author of that immortal work 'The Complete Angler', or 'The Contemplative Man's Recreation'. But as the Garden had its serpent, so does the Vale. It was here in the sleepy little village of Armathwaite in the winter of 1871 that the entire shanty town of Irish navvies erupted in riot. Sever damage was done to property, but most serious of all, one man was killed and injuries done to a score. Several navvies were placed on trial for murder.

This area in the eastern part of Westmoreland has long been renowned as a racing track for northbound expresses, and who are we, with nearly fifty miles of descent through the gorge of the River Eden, to break with tradition? The journey affords us kaleidascopic glimpses of deep furrowed valleys carving into the Pennines, with glorious views of the Eden winding amid the thickly wooded slopes. This particular stretch of line has always captured my interest no matter how many times I travel along it.

More cuttings follow through Barron Wood, with the river coming quite near to the line. The railway skirts round the side of the valley, the sleepers clinging tightly to the sandstone; according to which side of the cab one looks out, the train appears to be in a cutting or perched on the very edge of a precipice. I marvel at the herculean labours of the men who carved the way for the iron road. Three short tunnels, a cutting so deep that our smoke has just about disappeared before it can reach the top, and then we steam across the majestic nine-arched viaduct of Armathwaite. A succession of bridges and smaller viaducts then await us, before a short climb to the Low House Crossing. Finally, with the regulator closed we coast through Peteril Bridge and past the old derelict engine sheds of Durran Hill.

By now our speed has dropped to 20mph and the fireman wants to know why we are going backwards. He's only joking, of course, but the change in the sensation of power coming from the engine is so dramatic. We crawl so slowly past the London Road Junction signal box that there's almost time for a cuppa. Then round the right-hand curve, past the speed restriction markers, and finally we glide into Carlisle Citadel Station. Tired and hungry, we are more than ready for the bath which awaits us at the train crews' hostel at Upperby.

We have just shared a typical summertime trip, amidst such sylvan scenery, and with a beautiful locomotive beneath one's hand. But what of the other side of the track, so to speak?

A wintertime journey is one of extreme discomfort, even allowing for the presence of the fire. The bitterly cold winds which howl and slice across the open fells make life aboard a footplate an endurance test, taxing to the utmost, stamina, mental tenacity, and skill. The metal structure of the cab seems, with damnable perversity, to absorb more of the wintry climate than the welcome heat from the firebox. As one gets colder and colder, the rawness seeps into the very marrow of the bones, until the driver who occasionally peers from the cabside is little more than a petrified image. The footplate doors do not stay secure for long, as the forceful wind continually rattles them wide open, leaving the unfortunate crew with a mass of painful purple bruises as mementoes. It is not unknown for van tops to have been ripped off by the vicious sucking wind, to be flung, as though a mere cardboard packet, some considerable distance beyond the trackside.

The stretch of track between Hellifield and Aisgill is notorious among railwaymen. The rails climb northbound for several miles almost in a straight line up a gradient of 1 in 100; it is no surprise to learn that crews have nicknamed it, almost hatefully, as the 'Long Drag'. It used to be a common occurrence for trains to be stranded in snow drifts for thirty-six hours and more.

One of the most famous (or infamous) phenomena in this area is the Helm Wind. This starts at the top of Helm Fell, a soughing wind which soon becomes a miniature cyclone, literally roaring through the fells, flattening everything in its path. Woe betide any unfortunate sheep caught in its path; as they graze peacefully, blissfully unaware of impending disaster, they are just picked up and hurled aside by the wind. Broken limbs or loss of life are the usual outcome, winter and summer alike.

For myself and other train crews on the Carlisle run there was always the pleasant prospect of the Upperby hostel. But a job is never over until it is done, and unlike the passengers who can step from the train and immediately forget that it ever existed, the train crew's duties do not finish as soon as the locomotive pulls into Number One platform. Oh no. Almost from the very first days of railway there have been, in the Company's Rule Book, a set of rules and regulations governing procedure at the end of a journey. And in all cases, those rules have to be obeyed—inflexibly.

On arrival at Carlisle Upperby sheds, and that was quite a job to get from the main line to the yard tracks, I would report to the locomotive superintendent or to the shed foreman. But first, I had to carefully examine the engine, paying particular attention to valves and pistons, etc. My report would make note of any time lost and the reasons for the same, any accident to the locomotive or to the train however occasioned, and the nature of any defects or obstructions on the line, with signals, or other irregularities my fireman or myself had observed during the course of our journey.

The last of the day's footplate work was to drive my engine to its appointed place, after the fireman had dropped the fire and raked the ash-pan clean over the pit. With the regulator locked properly shut, the engine out of gear, brakes on, and the boiler filled with water ready for the next run, the day was nearly over. With the driver's report book dutifully filled in, an account of the day's work performed by the engine, and a daily return submitted to the foreman, my mate and I could sign off duty. At last we could pay heed to the tempting call of a bath and a meal at the hostel.

Situated at the top of a hill—never did a climb seem so long, almost as bad as the 'Drag'!—the Upperby hostel is a relatively new complex. While it is not up to five-star hotel standards, by comparison some other hostels in which I have stayed are very primitive indeed. Each person is allocated to a private cubicle which, though sparsely furnished, is basically comfortable. A bed, two chairs, a small set of drawers, and an occasional table are the standard furnishings. On the table is the inevitable Bible. One gets the impression that railwaymen are an evil lot—I reckon that they are beyond redemption anyway!—and the Bible is a kind of "ease thy conscience" inducement.

Upperby offers the luxury of several bathrooms, each fitted with a shower, which are a veritable Paradise after a gruelling trip. One can linger in a tub of hot water, relaxing tired muscles and soaking grimy limbs in the suds, or have a lovely refreshing shower to cleanse and tone up the whole body. Following a brisk rub down, one is ready to do full justice to the meal which awaits.

The food was quite reasonable, although most wise firemen refrained from eating the sweet course. Invariably it appeared on the menu as sponge

Carlisle Upperby shed on 26th November, 1964.   *(Norman Preedy)*

pudding. Believe me, if one had a plateful of this immediately prior to going on duty, then it was not long before the effects made themselves painfully felt. For example, soon after leaving Carlisle a fireman would start building up his fire, carefully placing lumps of coal all round the box against the walls, and lining the centre. Such endeavour on the part of the fireman called for plenty of action, most of it performed in a crouching position. Sponge puddings tend to lie rather heavily in one's stomach, and the crouching position seems to encourage an even firmer siting of the soggy mass. So much so, that the weight feels to have increased tenfold, causing great difficulty to the fireman when he tried to stand upright. A feeling of considerable discomfort followed which was not exactly conducive to the efficient firing of a great locomotive.

During the time in which I was familiar with Carlisle Upperby it had a fine recreation room with facilities for snooker and billiards, darts and dominoes, etc., comfortable lounge chairs were in abundance for those who preferred the less energetic pursuits of reading or just plain watching. The room also used as a forum by the trainmen who wished to air their views on every conceivable topic of conversation. Heated debates could be heard on such divergent themes as football, dog-racing, and the eventful or otherwise journeys on the way to Carlisle.

One source of amusement was indulged in by 'rabble rousing' passenger train guards. A seemingly quite innocent greeting from one to the other would be, "What sort have you worked up today, Joe?" On receiving an answer, the questioning guard would turn to the driver and the fireman of the same train, asking, ''What have you come up with?''. The question to the first guard was really loaded, since the driver and fireman had provided the means of his arrival, and any complaints he may have had about the journey were taken as an implied criticism of them. Many is the time that this has led to heated words between a train's crewmen, much to the amusement of the other train crews. Especially if he had had a particularly rough journey, the fireman could be relied on to give the offending guard a tongue lashing.

The situation puts me in mind of the perhaps aprocryphal tale of the hurried traveller who wished to make certain of catching a tight scheduled connection from another station. He had a few confidential words with the guard, urging him to ensure that the train left according to the time-table. Finally, a 'consideration' changed hands. Inevitably the train was late upon arrival at the connecting station, and the other train had departed. The irate traveller complained to the driver of his train, explaining that he had given fiscal encouragement to the guard. The driver listened stone-faced to the tirade, calmly wiping his hands on some cotton-waste. Then, coolly, he replied, ''Sorry mate, but you greased the wrong axle.''

After a good night's sleep and a nourishing breakfast at the hostel, let me take you on a typical return run from Carlisle. For this particular trip let us imagine the locomotive to be one of the 'Jubilee' Class 5X's, a powerful 4-6-0 first introduced by Stanier in 1934.

My fireman and I make our way down to the engine shed where the engine arrangement board tells us about the 'Jubilee'. We read closely any notices giving details of permanent way work in operation over the road we are about to travel. A trip to the locomotive stores enables us to draw firing shovel and irons, a bucket of spanners, a detonator case complete with flags and 'bangers', and then we make our way across to the engine. There she stands, sleek and sturdy, a 'rarin' to go; she looks lovely to me in the early light. While I stow the gear in the various boxes and racks, and deposit our personal equipment on board, my fireman nips back to the stores for a supply of oil, leaving me to drool over the lady, with admiration oozing out of every pore. He returns, and I set about oiling the engine, paying particular attention to cylinders, valves, and slides.

While I am doing this, my mate is spreading the fire evenly over the firebox grate and then building up with coal. There are several methods of firing, and experience, together with knowledge of the engine, tells him which to use. But all the methods have one thing in common, and that is system. Efficient building of a fire is a gradual process, and in between stages the fireman takes the opportunity to fill the paraffin lamps and trim the wicks, to clean the boiler gauge glasses and brasses, and to tidy up in general.

Soon the fire is in need of more coal; this is added, and in consequence the level of coal in the tender is diminished considerably. But preparation such as this is vitally necessary, especially if the crew wish to have a good trip home rather than a bad one. By now, I have finished my own preparations, and between us we take the 'Jubilee' under the coal chute for topping up purposes, and when the fireman has cleaned up, the water tank is filled up.

We are ready (almost), and now is the time for off. There is one important duty to attend to first, and that is to collect our train. We trundle off the shed tracks and go to join the carriages which patiently wait in the station. The fire is good and hot and the dampers are partly closed so that we are venting only a minimum of smoke. Partly closed dampers also ensure that the locomotive does not blow excessive steam through the safety valves. By maintaining the water level in the boiler at about the halfway mark the injectors can be used to add more water if the necessity arises. There is nothing worse than an engine standing in a station blowing off steam and wasting water and coal; it upsets me to see it.

There is still plenty of time in hand before our departure, as we back up, couple the shackle and fasten the vacuum pipes together. My fireman is doing all this while the guard gives me the particulars of the train, the number of coaches and their total weight; he also confirms the stops to be made en-route. On the way back to his compartment the guard also checks that the couplings have been made correctly and all doors fastened. Then we await the signal to go.

There is much whistle blowing from the station staff (it almost sounds like Saturday afternoon at United's ground) and with an answering 'toot' from the engine, away we go. The long haul over Shap summit has begun. The fireman opens the dampers and starts to fire, while I, holding the regulator open, look back along the train to see if all is well and everything is following in proper order. The train snakes out of Carlisle Citadel Station on time and heads south.

It is rather a laborious pull to Plumpton and it is raining hard. I am huddled in the corner of the cab, peering through the slashing needles of water while my mate is busy firing the engine. The rain lashes in between the aperture of the footplate roof and the tender, drenching the fireman in a steady downpour; he curses the day that he was foolhardy enough to join the Railway, and even dafter for wanting to be a fireman. But the rain, however persistent, eventually becomes something that he can endure, if not tolerate.

Despite all these trials and tribulations, all is going well as we reach Plumpton, and then the road begins to level out as we head towards Penrith Station. In between these two points I have gently coaxed her into a gallop, and we are touching up to 70mph. I close the regulator steadily to get round the Penrith curve and it feels as if I am physically pulling her round the rails at the slightly slower speed necessary, a mere 60mph. By now the fireman has his fire just right in readiness for the tortuous climb up

Shap. We successfully negotiate the Penrith Station stretch and I throw the regulator wide open. the '5X' roaring around the curves of Eden Vale Junction.

The feel of a powerful, man-sized, living locomotive beneath one's hand is something that can never be adequately described to, or understood by, the layman. It is an experience of a lovely steaming, oily smelling, clanking, snorting, monstrous mass of metal. The experience arouses different emotions in different railmen; and yet for each it is the same. The steam, the hot oil, and yes, even the soot and muck, flow through the brain and vein as surely as life-blood. The love and adoration which steam evokes is not a thought about which the railman or enthusiast consciously and deliberately ponders. Rather it is a sensation within oneself of which, from time to time, one becomes aware.

This awareness is upon me now, and I break out into a glorious rendering (that's what it sounds like to me!) of 'Keep right on to the end of the road'. My begrimed and long-suffering fireman is obviously not a patron of the choral arts. It's a good job those murderous looks of his cannot really kill! I charm him with a grin as we pound through the glades of trees to Thrimby Grange. With a steady beat we leave the sound of our passing echoing through the cement works on the right. Harrison sidings slip by, and our speed has dropped to 35 miles per hour.

But now, we gradually pick up speed, and soon the sweating fireman will enjoy a well-earned reprieve for his labours; Shap Station is passed and the long haul is ended. Our speed has risen and we are pounding along at about 60 miles per hour across the level stretch to Shap Summit. I ease the regulator across and finally close it as we begin the descent of the one in seventy-five Shap Fell gradient. My fireman now has the chance to take a well-earned lid of tea; for some time he's had it keeping warm, balanced precariously on the hotplate above the firehole door. I'd like to join him, but just now I've got to keep my eyes on the road ahead, and a tight leash on the engine.

Soon the speed is hitting the eighties and the '5X' is rolling like a frigate on the high seas. Indeed, it will not be long before we look like a ship knifing through the waves. To anyone standing on the platform at Tebay the sight of the '5X' coming down the bank was little, if anything, short of majestic. I am sure that they would bear me out when I say it was one of the finest spectacles that one could wish to see. If they had the good fortune, as I now have, to ride on the footplate, they would agree that it would be an even greater thrill.

But even when one is part of such majesty, and when one is trembling with the thrill sublime as much as with the rolling footplate, duty still makes its insistent call. The somewhat quaint little country junction station at the foot of Shap trembles at our approach and almost seems to cringe as we flash through like a fiery bolt from Hades. The fireman has no eyes for the passing scene for he is standing by the water scoop handle ready to take

44

on water at the troughs.

They are made of thick steel plate pressed to the required shape and assembled in sections. In position they lie upon longitudinal sleepers secured to the normal permanent way sleepers and lie snug between the rails. There is no heating system incorporated to keep the water from freezing during cold weather.

There is a sudden tenseness in the cab; although we are belting along like the clappers, it is almost as if time has stood still . . . "Right", I shout, the sound of my voice, for a split second, drowning the metalic roar of the engine. As if electrified, my fireman drops the scoop to pick up some 2500 gallons of water. Instantly it is as if the mighty locomotive has gone at speed right off the end of the Blackpool Pier! We are surrounded by water. A sheet of water about twenty feet high froths and plumes back along the train for about four coach lengths, dying away to a fine spray which spatters over the remaining coaches. Once again I bellow a command—"Up", and the water scoop is back in position, ready for the next time. The roaring sound of the violently agitated water has gone, presumably to join the fine spray mist swirling in our slipstream, now the only record of our passing. I offer a silent vote of thanks to the memory of James Ramsbottom, who has enabled us to continue our run the easier, through the invention of the water trough for use by the railways in 1860.

Of course, we didn't hit the troughs at 80 miles per hour, but having slowed to about 60 miles per hour, we now need to increase our speed to cope with the slightly rising gradient to Low Gill. Immediately we clear the troughs I open the regulator again, and the fireman's back is bent once more to the strenuous task of feeding coal into the open mouth of the ever-hungry firebox.

Past Low Gill, we begin the fast descent again and over on the right is seen the fine view of the town of Kendal. Some say that the best view is obtained from the platform of Oxenholme station; I do not agree, but I admit that I am biased, since I reckon that there is nothing to compare with the view from the footplate. However, I acknowledge that the old London and North Western system of railways from Oxenholme Junction afforded an easy and delightful means of access to the beautiful Lake District. The exquisite beauty of this District, its variety of seasonal colouring, and its endless charms are best described by the eloquence of the poets. I commend them to you.

The line pursues its way past Milnethorpe station before we roar through Burton and Holme at 90 miles per hour. We flash through Carnforth Junction, getting a brief glimpse of the engine sheds on the right and the network of tracks that make up the marshalling yards. The rapid growth and increase in importance of Carnforth, set in bold and magnificent scenery, was due to its participation in the iron trade of the district, a trade in turn being largely occasioned by the advent of the railways.

The fireman is standing by the water scoop once more, in readiness for the Hest Bank Troughs. "Down", I yell, and another tankfull of water is taken on board. But this time the fireman has difficulty with the water scoop which is hard to pull up against the water pressure created by our forward motion. It remains in the down position when the tank is full.

In a split-second of awareness I notice all this as I pay heed to the road ahead and the controls of the locomotive. I know what is about to happen, but it is too late to do anything, even if I could. The scoop remains extended and consequently the water rushes up the gauge and cascades over the fireman. Gallons of water over flow from the back of the tender, its floodtide sweeping the coal onto the footplate. The poor fireman, with as fine a range of good old Anglo-Saxon expletives as anyone could wish to hear, blesses the scoop and its ancestry. Needless to say, I grinning like a Cheshire cat at the plight of the unfortunate man, am the main target of his displeasure!

But order is soon once more restored to the footplate; we have work on our hands as the train hurtles around Morecambe Junction. We are now turning away from the view of Morecambe Bay, which at high tide is a fine sheet of water eight or ten miles wide. Like a hound off the leash, the '5X' is headed for Lancaster Castle—not literally of course, since this strong fortress, erected by John o'Gaunt in the reign of Edward III, stands atop of a hill to the west of the town. Up the short but steep Lancaster Bank, with thunderous coughs of steam as we streak through the station at 60 miles per hour, before cresting the Bank and around the wide sweeping curve at Lancaster No. 1.

I open wide the regulator and adjust the cut-off to the cylinders to somewhere around the 40% mark—but what's this? What is happening? I am getting the wrong response from the engine. With a hasty look out to the driving wheels and the coupling rods I see they are merely thrashing around instead of being an almost hypnotic blur. In far less time than it has taken to tell, the fireman and I are already aware of what is happening, knowing that a glance at the steam gauge will only confirm our recognition of the symptoms. The needle has started to drop and is now hovering around the 190psi mark.

My fireman has opened the fire-door, and by means of the shovel has detected the cause of our trouble. Using the shovels blade as a deflector the air is directed towards the area of the fire to be examined. As it passes forward as a flameless current it presents a clear view of the fire for inspection. My mate can now see where fresh coal is needed most, and he promptly begins to place a few extra shovelsful in any holes he has observed by this tactic. But this is not the complete answer, for the steam gauge shows the pressure of steam still gradually dropping.

This means that there is some clinker clogging the fire-bars. So the fireman grabs the fire-iron known as the chisel dart. This is about seven or eight feet long with the business end tapering down to something like an arrow head or multi-sided chisel-hence the name. It is inserted into the fire and used as a lever to break up any unwanted solid masses of unburnt coal; this action frees the bars and secures the good draught necessary for rapid combustion. The whole manouvre is extremely hot and the sweat pours off him. In the best traditions of countless generations of stokers he is lamenting the day that he ever started in railway service. But his sterling efforts are proving effective—we are recovering. There are clouds of smoke coming from the front end, and the steam pressure is once again holding its own.

For a little while, the fire is allowed to burn without the addition of any coal, but after this short time has elapsed, the fireman takes up the shovel again and deflects the air around the firebox. Any holes that he still sees by this process are filled up with small coal, and he takes this opportunity to work off the small lumps which have trickled to the front of the tender. The results are successful and the needle starts to creep up until the gauge is reading 225psi Maximum. The fireman has won his battle.

We have both had reminders concerning the secret of good firing. For myself, that the driver should always keep an eye on the fire whenever possible; and for the fireman, that he should fire frequently, a little at a time, preferably with the steam 'on'. It requires patience and perseverance, but in the long run it is the only way to accomplish hours of hard travelling with anything like succes. Many schemes have been used for increasing firing efficiency and making good steam; but the best plan has always been the employment of intelligent firemen who understand the principles affecting combustion, and who also know their locomotive.

While the fire-box drama has been enacted, I too, have been playing a vital role. All the herculean efforts of my mate would have been wasted had I not been nursing the engine. By just having the regulator opened slightly, and the cut-off being at the minimum, the power has been allowed to build up again while we have trundled along.

We must surely have lost some time during all this, probably as much as four minutes, or about six miles short of schedule. But now we are fully recovered as we rush through Garstang. So with a wide open regulator and the cut-off down to the 'D' mark, we start to fly along once more in an effort to make up time. Unfortunately this means that if lost time is to be regained I cannot be as economical with the coal as I would wish.

Barton and Broughton are passed two minutes late— perhaps with a bit of luck this can be regained before Preston. The speedo' reads 80 miles per hour and all seems to be well. But as we pass Oxheys we run into adverse signals, so quickly the speed is brought down to about 25 miles per hour. It's a funny thing about reducing speed from something as high as 80, but time seems to stand still until one begins to wonder if the shuddering monster beneath one's feet is really under control. Everything is alright this time and I slow the engine down to 20 miles per hour. We coast into Preston Station No. 6 platform one minute late. Not too bad, all things being considered.

Our relief crew climbs aboard and we give them a brief report of the run and the performance of the engine. After the signing of the log-book, and a words of good-natured banter, my fireman and I climb down. I take a quick look at the '5X' to see that she is alright—the new crew will give her a thorough inspection before moving out again—and with my mate I walk away. Both of us are tired, dirty, and thirsty, but happy and content with a job well done.

All that now remains to be done is to book off duty and seek out an hostelry wherein to wet our parched throats. As we take our seats for the pleasant task which lies ahead, I hasten to draw the fireman's attention to a simple fact which he appears to have overlooked—it is the usual custom for the fireman to buy the first round. Fixing me with baleful glare, and delivering a choice of words like an affronted Oracle (levelled at me, of course), he pays up with as good a grace as he can muster. The reluctant purchased pint of beverage is soon disposed of and I need no prompting to get the next round of drinks.

We are soon joined by our colleagues and naturally enough the conversation is not long in turning to engines and railways. "What sort of trip did you have?" I, of course replied, "Not bad." My fireman nods a deprecating head at me. "He doesn't tell you that she started to die approaching Oubeck and we didn't recover until passing Garstang. Apart from that and the water scoop sticking, we were in the pink."

There is laughter all round and plenty of banter. We hear other tales of the tracks. In their telling is the rare spice of an engineman's life. Another driver recounts his experience of the day, having had trouble of a different kind. He set out on a trip to Rose Grove with a train of sixty empty coal wagons, but due to a faulty coupling (a rare event), he and his mate had had to deal with a break-loose between the thirtieth and the thirty-first waggon.

And so the talk goes on, all of us enjoying a pleasant time among friendly company.

Chapter VI
HOME AND DISTANT.

At various times during 1957 I had toyed with the idea of moving to another depôt. I continually scanned the vacancy lists, and one day I noticed a vacancy for a driver of my seniority at Bidston. Bidston? I had no idea where it was, nor the type of work they had. A few discreet inquiries were made and I found this mysterious place to be in the Wirral/Liverpool area. A day off, and a trip in the car soon satisfied my curiosity if not my ambition.

I located the engine shed which consisted of two or three shed roads. That was enough for me. I promptly returned home, for there was no chance of my wanting to transfer there. My ambition lay with a depôt that had plenty of long distance work. So I bided my time but didn't entirely give up the idea of transferring. As the saying goes, "Good things are worth the waiting".

During this time, we at Lostock Hall were constantly losing work to other depôts. Not unexpectedly, this state of affairs had an adverse effect upon the morale of the men, particularly among those in my seniority group. We were not getting our usual Carlisle jobs, and the coal trains from Crofton Hall were being worked by Wakefield men. Similarly, a large number of our Blackpool and Heysham jobs were being taken over by the Preston depôt. A sorry state of affairs which could only end in the complete demoralising of the crews. The writing was on the wall for Lostock Hall.

If things continued in this unsatisfactory fashion it would not be very long before we finished up as we had started, a mere level crossing. (The Hall had been a very dangerous level crossing which was replaced sometime around 1856 by a bridge; a booking hall was actually built into the bridge. The station was built during the year 1888, and the Lostock Junction was widened by powers granted in the Parliamentary Act of 1892.)

Men from Newton Heath were now coming to our depot to work the Manchester trains, while we had to be satisfied with all the shunting and short trip jobs. This was bad for our self-esteem, mine especially, as I had always had a good route card and was extremely proud of this fact, but as a result of the changed diagramming, it was of no use to me—I was confined to local work and sundry shunting jobs. Rather ironic, looking back on it, to think that there had been a time in my career when I had been as pleased as a dog with two tails to do shunting. It was the accumulative effect of this state of affairs which prompted my thoughts again to seriously considered a move to another depot. Only one small problem needed to be solved first. Which one?

I continually 'pumped' the men from Preston about their depot, and likewise the men from Carlisle. I weighed up the information I thus received most carefully; after all, not only had I to consider myself and the possibilities of future advancement, but also my wife. She would, like other womenfolk, play an important part in a move such as I was contemplating. As the wives of almost any enginemen will tell you, their social life is severely restricted due to the irregularity of their husbands' shifts. Working hours which start at half-past two in the morning and finish sometime around the conventional lunch-time are most definitely anti-social. On such a shift I would arrive home at half-twelve and go straight into a hot bath. After that luxurious and most welcome soak, I would have a meal, read the papers, and retire to bed for a few hours much-needed sleep. By then it was getting on for three o'clock.

Anyone who has had experience of trying to sleep in the daytime will know that it can be one of the hardest jobs in the world. The effort! The distractions! There always seems to be someone with a special dislike for you. The coalman on his delivery rounds seems to be wearing newly-studded boots as he walks up freshly laid concrete or gravel paths; surely the next-door neighbours don't have ten tons of stuff delivered every day? Milkmen seem to be delivering their bottles in the manner of an American newspaper boy; and the corporation refuse collectors, having hurled half of the dustbins into the lorry, sound as if they are trying to imitate the most novice Jamaican steel band with the rest. It goes almost without saying that all the kids in the entire estate neighbourhood are competing to see who can scream the loudest; or perhaps they are trying to deaden the sound of a battery of radios blasting out 'pop' numbers at full belt.

All these things are not in the least bit conducive to a few hours well-earned sleep. It was not uncommon for me to step out of bed with temper frayed raw, ready to do battle with anyone and anything who dared to cross my path. Of course, my nearest and dearest was the first in the firing line and took the brunt of it all. My wife, bless her heart, took it all with remarkable equanimity, and she used to say to me after some little row, "Never mind Bert, it will soon be the week-end, and you'll be on a good turn next week."

I would soon subside, and together we would watch a television show. Then it would be back to bed again until about half-past one in the morning, when a new day would dawn for me, long before the sun was awake.

I was still busily pursuing my work-time diversion of scanning the vacancy lists for a suitable shed when, one day, I was called to the foreman's office. "There's a job at Preston Station to Crewe, so go down there and report to Preston Control."

Those were my orders. Simple enough, but their effect upon me was to change my life yet again. Another set of tracks for me to learn, and yet more columns to be filled on the route card of my experience.

I was informed by Control, the 'Brains' as we used to call them, that my train was a rake of cattle waggons from Carlisle en route for Shrewsbury. With my fireman I took her into Crewe, where on our arrival we were relieved by another train crew. This gave me the opportunity to look at

Crewe North shed. What I was able to see there convinced me that if I was to transfer anywhere, Crewe it would be.

There were in the region of forty-eight shed roads filled with all types of locos. I felt as if I had been let loose in a railway style Aladdin's cave. There were 'Duchesses' and Class '5's', Great Western 'Castles' and 'Halls', and Midland Class '4's'. Already I was beginning to tremble with excitement at the prospect of a move here. But I kept the lid on my bubbling enthusiasm, and my thoughts to myself. That is, until one day I noticed a vacancy at Crewe, and it was for a driver of my seniority!

I could scarcely contain myself when I went home. I said, trying to be casual, "Norah, how would you like to go and live at Crewe. There is a driver vacancy there."

Her reply was immediate. "When do we go?" This took the steam right out of my boiler, "If you want to go to Crewe, then Crewe it is." I hugged and kissed her, speechless.

So the decision was made. I filled in the necessary transfer forms and awaited events. On the 16th August, 1959 the results of the interviews were posted. My name was underlined as the successful applicant.

I had been accepted at Crewe and a fortnight later I reported for duty to 'His Highness', the Divisional Superintendent. During this fortnight of waiting—it felt like a year—I seemed to come into contact with more Crewe men than ever I had done before. Naturally enough, most of my conversations with them were filled with questions about Crewe, the predominant one being, "What type of work will I be doing on arrival there?"

The answers filled me with dismay. The information which seemed to burn into my brain was that young drivers started their careers in the shunting yards. I was in absolute torment and my thoughts ran wild. "What on earth have I done?" "Have I made a mistake?" I had wanted to leave Lostock Hall because of too many shunt jobs and local trips, but now that I had taken the fateful plunge and decided to move, I was about to step right into a link doing nothing else but shunt.

With my mind in such a whirl, there was only one thing to do. Ask my dad. He was an old railwayman and he would know what was what. He listened patiently while I poured out my tale of woe, and his answer, which seemed to ignore my feelings about the whole affair, was like a douche of cold water. I fear that I got little consolation from his words, for all that he said to me was, "Well son, you made the decision, and now you'll have to abide by it. So stop feeling sorry for yourself. Go and get on with it."

They were words of wisdom indeed, although at the time I could not appreciate that simple fact. That night when I went to bed sleep was right out of the question. I tossed and turned and dozed fitfully. When it was time to get up my head felt as though a dozen 'Royal Scots' had been running over and through it. I was in a terrible state as I went to report for duty.

My mate at this time was driver George Whalley, and a more practical man never breathed. He took one look at me, and with a voice tinged with gentle cynicism, said, "Bert, the way you look this morning, you'll never make Crewe. We shall have to have a whip-round for a wreath. What kind of flowers would you like?"

His words served to shake me a little out of my apathy. After the day's work we went to the Railway Hotel just across the road from the shed. I had thought to drown my sorrows which had welled up inside me again. But once more, driver Whalley came to the rescue. "You don't drown your sorrows, Bert. You only teach them to swim." Yet again he had given me the benefit of some priceless philosophy.

He really gave me a good talking-to, sparing neither my blushes nor my wounded pride. Outlining the many advantages of moving to a place like Crewe, he pointed out that I should not always be on the shunt links. He talked of the mileage jobs as the big'uns, and the flair I possessed to do these jobs. For a period of about two days he really laid it on the line for me, working at me until me doubts had been resolved and my self-confidence restored. I was now able to view the future objectively and without apprehension.

I can never forget dear old George, nor thank him enough for all he did for me in this important phase in my career. I consider that he, and enginemen like him are the embodiment of the true gentlemen of the footplate. They are the real salt of the earth.

During this time, I had managed to do a little reading up on the subject of Crewe, in order that, knowing a little of the history of the place, I could enter into its spirit more easily.

In the golden days of its glory there can hardly have been a busier railway station in the country than Crewe. More than six hundred trains per day passed through its control. In other words, more than one train every two and a half minutes was pounding along its tracks. It was the principal junction of the London and North Western system. The locomotive works extended for nearly two miles and were situated in the fork of lands between the Liverpool and Chester/Holyhead lines.

The town itself grew up as a direct result of the development of the London and North Western Railway Company. On July 4th, 1837, the first train passed through what was then a village of less than one hundred and fifty people. The railway was then called the Grand Junction Railway. An amalgamation later in that same year between the Manchester & Liverpool, the Manchester & Birmingham, the London & Birmingham, and other lines, gave rise to the LNWR. In August, 1842, the new line was opened to the public. The Board of Directors of the new Company were not slow to see that Crewe was admirably situated in a central position. It was obvious that several lines must converge there, and that it would thus become a great meeting-place for railways. The excellent site gave promise as being suitable for the construction of locomotives and rolling stock. Accordingly, in 1843, the Grand Junction Works at Edge Hill, Liverpool, were transferred to Crewe. From that time the development of the town began, with the Railway Company being the largest employer of local labour in the area.

The first Locomotive Superintendent was Mr. F. Trevithick, the son of the great Trevithick who in 1805 exhibited his 'steam coach' in Euston Square, near the site later occupied by the famous Doric Arch, so shamefully demolished in the 1970's by British Rail. The Company's total stock of locomotives at the time of his appointment was only seventy-five. Successive Chiefs of Mechanical Engineering at Crewe developed its resources to quite a remarkable extent. The works became almost entirely self-sufficient, comprising General Offices, Photographic Studio, Steel Mills, and Rolling Plant. Just prior to the turn of the century the North Western was the only English railway company that rolled its own rails. Other facilities included in this vast railway factory complex were the Foundries, Paint Shop, Locomotive Erecting and Repair Works, and Saw Mills. The establishment at Crewe justly proud of its ability to supply the needs for the whole of the Company's network. To think I was now about to be plunged into this rich melting pot of railway history.

On the 30th August, 1959, I bade farewell to Lostock Hall and all its wonderful associations. I reported in at Crewe North shed, and on entering the drivers' lobby enquired for the shed foreman. I was directed to him, and introduced myself to foreman Jennings, stating that I came from Lostock Hall.

Heads turned at my statement. "Lostock Hall? Where on earth is that?" Some wag called across the room, "Don't you know? That's the place where they still use jungle drums instead of telephones." I could feel my face beginning to burn, but the smiles of good humour on the faces of the chaps around me took the sting from their words and saved me from letting go with a mouthful of Anglo-Saxon repartee! I put on a sheepish grin and the tension was gone. Within a few minutes I was escorted on a tour of the North shed and the Old Works. This latter was so dark and dismal that it had earned the nickname of 'Abyssinia'. From there I went to see the Staff Clerk who recorded a few personal details and gave me my number—502. It was this which made me realise the vast difference between Crewe and my former shed. It was a world apart from Lostock Hall where my number had been 106.

At this particular time the Crewe North and South sheds had a complement of well in excess of 1000 men, excluding the artisan staff and their labourers. One of these chaps was an inveterate pipe smoker who was renowned. A firebox would need the brick arch rebuilding, and inevitably before crawling inside the box he would light up his pipe. In the confines of the firebox he would proceed to choke his mate. It used to be reckoned that there was more smoke coming out of the firebox at such times than if the fire had been lit for 'steam up'.

I had chummed up with a chap from Wigan Springs Branch, Bill Norburn by name—a real character. Like myself, he had been transferred. Our first job was to get thoroughly acquainted with the North shed roads. As I recall, we were walking along the tracks some two hundred yards outside the shed towards the shed outlet, when . . . "Hey up".

At the sound of this bellowing voice Bill instinctively jumped two sets of rails to the left. Similarly, I took evasive action to the right, fully expecting a locomotive to be bearing down on us. Happily, this was not the case.

We looked around for the owner of the stentorian voice and saw a fellow walking towards us. He was another transferee from Westhouses as we learned after introductions. Apparently, "Hey up", is the customary method of approach when wishing to speak with folks. He gave his name as Reg Wilson, but this was never used by Bill or myself thereafter. Indeed, by one and all at Crewe, he was known as "Hey up". The three of us 'clicked' together at once. We joined forces, doing everything together, so much so that we earned the collective nickname of 'Freeman, Hardy and Willis'.

Together we learned the roads, motive traction (in this case 350hp shunting diesels), and the thousand and one other things which made Crewe tick. We even got digs together in the town. In this we were unfortunate. Our living quarters were little, if anything, better than the hovels in which the railway navvies had existed. Three single beds, three chairs, all of indifferent comfort, a small table, and a miniature cooker for the preparation of our meals, were our meagre furnishings. In this thoroughly depressing place heating arrangements were practically non-existent. The bedroom was so cold that icicles hung from the roof beams, but we had to endure these conditions since we had no alternative at the time, although there was room for us at the trainmens' hostel in Gresty Road, but the shed boss had stipulated that we could not stay there for more than two days. It was this instruction that first brought me face to face, as it were, with the pettiness of 'bumbledom' and railway politics.

We had been in digs for about three weeks when we were all summoned to the boss's office. He informed us that three railway houses had just come up for re-letting. "You are each being paid expenses, three pounds a week, so it has been decided that you are to have these houses." We were not asked if we would like to have them, instead we were told in most definite terms that we had to move in. This angered us, but we said nothing.

To cut an unpleasant story short, we decided to go along with the instruction, and view these houses. Houses? I use the term loosely; hovels more like. There was no hot water system in any, lighting was by gas in the Victorian style, and the communal toilet was situated some fifteen yards or so from the buildings. We scarcely said a word, we were too dumbfounded, but our resolve was unanimous. On our return we went to the shed boss and told him, in equally definite terms what he could do with the houses. His action at our reply startled us, to say the least. He ranted and raved, banged the desk with his clenched fist, but we held fast. Calmly we told him that we were each making private negotiations, and that we would make our own decisions where to live and in what sort of dwelling. The choice of environment would be ours, not his, nor that of anyone else. This only served to inflame him more. Through another violent spasm he talked of suspending us immediately. Quite plainly this was victimisation, so we made consultation with the branch secretary of the union, the Associated Society of Locomotive Engineers and Firemen (ASLEF). But before we and the union could get together to discuss the problem, the boss apologised for his behaviour and made his peace with us. Thus ended the only really unpleasant episode in my entire career.

In the space of two months my two pals had been housed to their satisfaction; my own bungalow was in the process of being built. Almost literally, I watched it go up brick by brick, as every Friday night I would visit the site to see how work was progressing. It was the first 'home of our own', so I was eager to move in, and I pestered the life out of the site foreman to build it a bit faster. Whether or not my harassment had any effect I do not know, but one month later Norah and I moved into our bungalow. There were the usual problems at such a time—curtains, carpets, crocks, furniture, fixtures, and fittings—none of which seemed to be available at the right time or in the right place. But eventually we settled snugly into our new home.

I was particularly quiet one night when my wife asked if I had any problems on my mind. I replied that I had no domestic problems—"Merely conjuring with my thoughts and looking for opportunities to wangle my way into the money jobs." I didn't know the road to London, so as this was my Number One priority, I began to work on the foreman. After a lot of persuading he agreed to let me go out and learn the road. Lo, and behold! My two pals were also detailed to learn the same road, so we teamed up yet again.

It's one of the cardinal rules when learning the roads that one finds the nearest canteen and nearest fish and chip shop, nearest that is, to any of the likely stops en route. That being done, then the job of learning the roads becomes a lot easier.

The first stage we did was the road to Stafford and that was quickly learned. The stage was as far as Nuneaton. We agreed that the best way to do this one was by boarding a goods locomotive that was working a train from Crewe to Nuneaton. So this we did.

I asked the fireman if he would care to go and join the guard at the rear of the train. At my explanation that one of us would do the firing, he readily agreed. We set off with me doing my stuff with the shovel and as it is a pretty stiff climb from Crewe to Whitmore, just beyond Bunker's Hill cutting, it was no time at all before I was sweating profusely. This prompted the driver to comment, studiously avoiding looking at me, "The trouble is, these Lancs. and Yorks. firemen lead such sheltered lives, they are not used to hard work." My replies to this is strickly not for publication! However, despite the disparaging remarks concerning my ability, we topped the bank with a full head of steam. The tank was refilled on the Whitmore troughs, and we started to coast down all the way to Stafford. This famous boot and shoe manufacturing town is situated around what is still a fairly important junction and station. Here commences the Trent Valley loop line, now a part of the main line.

Awaiting the road south 'Coronation' 46232 'Duchess of Sutherland' stands in Stafford station with the 'Merseyside Express' on a sunny summer's day in 1961.
(Norman Preedy)

There was a slight delay at Stafford Station due to adverse signals; we had to await the passing of some express trains. As we chatted away on the footplate, the driver suddenly said, "Come on, one of you take her into Nuneaton." Bill Norburn immediately stepped into the driving position. Instantly, I hurled the shovel into the tender, and to the shocked and open-mouthed driver I said, "If you think I'm going to heave coal for him, you have another think coming." For a moment, I am sure, he thought that I meant it.

As I had made my remark to the driver, Bill had picked up the coal hammer and threatened to crack my skull with it. In mock terror I jumped off the footplate and ran down the platform with Bill in hot and vociferous pursuit. I bolted round the station building with Bill gaining at every step, and as we climbed back on board the loco, Bill had a firm hold of me by the scruff of the neck. An old lady broke from among some waiting passengers to give Bill the lenght of her tongue. For good measure she brought her umbrella down across his shoulders with a resounding 'Thwack'. By this time I was doubled up with laughter, and so were the driver and Reg Wilson. The only one without even a smile was poor old Bill. As you will have realised, the whole affair was a bit of horse-play, but the old lady thought that it was all for real; her reaction with the umbrella was purely spontaneous. God bless the old dear for trying to defend me.

To show that there was no ill-feeling I retrieved the shovel from the tender and started to build up the fire in preparation for our departure. Bill took the controls, and as we pulled slowly away from the platform and our captive audience, the militant Amazon, defender of the down-trodden, had a parting word with him.

"You leave him alone, you big bully", she yelled. In anticipation of another crack from the brolly which she still brandished, Bill hastily withdrew his head. The driver's comment was, "You two will get me paid up if she ever reports this incident." We all laughed.

We steamed away and as we approached Shugborough Tunnel Reg said to me, sotto voce, "Quick, open the tender doors before we enter the tunnel." Moving casually so as not to attract attention, I opened the doors and Reg went into the tender. I felt like a stage magician, no-one had noticed our actions, and strangest of all, no-one had observed the absence of Reg. Just about fifty yards inside the tunnel I took advantage of the almost total darkness to close the doors. The others did not have an inkling at all about what was happening.

We emerged from the tunnel in an explosive burst of smoke and steam, the suction of our passage drawing every sooty wraith from the depths of this subterranean gravel bore. I looked at Bill, I looked at the driver, and back again, horror written all over my face. "Where on earth is Reg?", I shouted. Panic and consternation quickly spread across their faces as their heads swivelled from side to side, vainly seeking the missing member of the crew. The reaction of reason almost immediately took charge of the panic, and Bill, in command of the situation prepared to stop the train.

Of course, I could not let this happen, so I opened the tender doors, and like a magician producing a rabbit, I revealed the white-eyed, blackened face of my fellow conspirator. Covered in coal-dust whipped up inside the tender by the tunnel's draught, he really looked like one of the performers from the Black and White Minstrel Show!

After the laughter had subsided somewhat, and the driver had swallowed all his murderous instincts, he said, "The sooner we ***** well arrive in Nuneaton, the better. Then I can get rid of you three. At this rate, you'll have me a nervous wreck before long." And so we settled down to learn the road.

The road to Nuneaton was fairly easy to learn as regards to the signalling system, loops, and the slight gradients. Once there however, the local layout and practices had to be learned. The criss-cross pattern of the numerous sidings had to be familiarised along with the engine sheds and their feeding roads. Shed procedures, the going on and coming off techniques, each one different, had to be acquired. However, we mastered all these moves, and the next stage to learn was between Nuneaton and Rugby.

As with the main line to Nuneaton, so it was with the tracks to Rugby—not too difficult. But at Rugby the scene was somewhat different. Situated on what had once been known as the Trent Valley Loop Line, the station area was a maze of tracks, with the post signals sprouting up all over the place, and the ground signals in such profusion that they almost littered the rails. Trap points facing road movements were in operation. This meant travelling on the 'wrong' line between one point and another, and as may well be imagined, this required needle-sharp concentration when performing such moves. These moves were often referred to as 'Bang road movements', since, if any mistake were to be made by either the driver or the signalman a collision could occur.

To learn the section south of Rugby we left the freight train and boarded the footplate of a 'flyer'. This was a Liverpool to London express hauled by a 'Royal Scot' class locomotive. Although, as I have recounted earlier, I had towed a 'Scottie', this was the first time that I had ever been on the footplate of one of these magnificent engines. Positioned behind the driver, I thoroughly enjoyed myself.

The fireman had said to Bill, when he gave up his seat, "I shan't have time to sit down when we leave Rugby." How right he was. As we left Stowe Hill Tunnel and thundered towards Roade Cutting and Junction at 80 miles per hour, he was continually shovelling coal into the hungry firebox.

By this time tears were streaming from my eyes as, with my head hanging over the footplate doors and trying to peer round the driver's head, I faced into the high velocity wind. The force of that wind was such that for a moment or two I really thought the sides of my eyes had been cut. We picked up water on the troughs at Castlethorpe and hurtled onwards towards Wolverton, our speed well over the 90 miles per hour mark. There is a permanent speed restriction in force here, strictly adhered to by the drivers, so as we went over the viaduct at Wolverton Carriage Works, the driver started to apply the brakes so as to go through Wolverton Station at 80 miles per hour. The speed restriction is necessary because of the succession of right-hand and left-hand curves. Safely round, and with the regulator open again, we flew towards our next destination stage—Bletchley. Here we took our leave from the 'Scottie' and her Liverpool crew; they had taught us much, and only time would show how well we learned.

There was a lot of railway to learn around Bletchley. Engine sheds, goods train sidings, special sidings for coaching stock, plus ground signals, trap points, 'wrong-road' movements; and while we're at it, "Where's the canteen?"

We took about the average time to learn the various procedures, which was four days. When we were confident of our individual knowledge to, and about Bletchley, we decided to move one stage nearer our goal of London Euston. This next stage along the iron road took us as far as Willesden.

Once again we boarded the footplate of a freight train and said farewell to Bletchley. This time we were on the Up Slow line, this being the usual procedure for goods trains. Our pace was slow as we passed through some very lovely Buckinghamshire countryside, with Leighton Buzzard and its graceful church spire, and over on the left, a range of chalk hills bordering the Dunstable Downs. On this particular day we saw none of the gliders for which Dunstable is famous, but looking closely at the hills we saw the famous lion carved into the hillside.

Our freight train ambled on south across the Vale of Aylesbury, passing Cheddington Junction, which was later to be the scene of the Great Train Robbery. From there we climbed up the bank, and by a deep cutting through the Chiltern Hills, crested the rise at Tring Station, from which point the fireman could relax a little as we coasted down-hill. Even so, we maintained a steady 50 miles per hour which was pretty good for a freight train.

The trackside and signals told us that we were on the approach roads to Willesden Junction. Even today, a glance at a map of the London district will show the tremendous importance of the place. It is a virtual artery through which a steady stream of trains connect with most parts of the country.

As we came nearer to the locomotive sheds and vast marshalling yards of Willesden we were checked at numerous signals; like every other train it was necessary that we took our turn inside the yard. Our driver informed us that if we had been fortunate the road would have been open for us to run right in. However, such was the volume trains that were dealt with there, we would have to wait—and that could take anything up to two or three hours. This was not on our list of priorities, nor to our benefit, so the three of us dropped off at Wembley, waved farewell to our mentors and companions, and caught a local train to Euston.

Being so far from our home depot we decided to stay overnight at the enginemens' hostel at Camden. First on the list for all of us was a nice hot bath followed by a welcome tea, then having satisfied the inner man, we did the rounds of the various enjoyments offered by the recreation room. As always, in between frames of snooker, games of dominoes, or hands of cards, I listen to and join in with the chat. Many men from different sheds, Liverpool, Carlisle, Manchester, and the like can create quite a hubbub of conversation, and some of them can really tell a tale. I wouldn't go so far as to say that the stories are untrue, but I am sure that they stretch the credibility gap about as far as the tracks they have just run; but they are very entertaining yarns so one does not mind very much.

One such amusing tale has always remained in my bank of memories. A driver, who shall be nameless, related a story of a train-hopping guard, who shall be equally anonymous. The guard had had a very rough trip in his van on a particular run, but the following day reported for duty as usual. He inspected the train and gave his report on its composition to the driver, and said, on taking his leave, "I'll see you at London, driver."

"O.K.", replied the driver as he went through his departure procedures, "Don't get lost."

The train pulled out, and when finally it arrived at Willesden the guard was already there. The driver was dumbfounded, and asked the guard how in hell he had managed to arrive before the train.

"Well", said the guard, "I told you that I had a rough trip yesterday. I wasn't going to have another one today, so I caught a passenger train and travelled in comfort instead."

Needless to say, his actions were reported, and British Rail dispensed with his services as a guard. I cannot vouch for the truth of the story, but certainly the former guard became a shunter at Rugby and in later years rose to the exalted rank of Station Foreman, in charge of the stabling of electric locomotives. Ah well! In the words of the Immortal Bard,

"But be not afraid of greatness: some men
are born great, some achieve greatness,
and some have greatness thrust upon them."

(Act II. v. Twelfth Night.)

The Camden hostel was known among railwaymen as the 'Bastille'. I had often wondered why, and that night I was to find out. We were allotted a room on the first floor which unfortunately overlooked the shunting room; it had looked peaceful enough when we first stowed our gear. But that night we were given a 'captive' performance by a 350hp diesel shunting loco beneath us. The noise was terrific, and the vibrations were so intense that one did not need to bother turning over in bed—this was done automatically by the loco! I don't think that I can really recommend British Rail's chamber-maid service. Sleep was out of the question—I've dozed off easier on the footplate. How ever railwaymen can claim to sleep under such duress I shall never know.

The next morning, somewhat bleary eyed, but perking up after a substantial breakfast at about six o'clock, we were ready to make our way to Willesden. Here we had to learn what is probably one of the largest marshalling yards between London and Carlisle. To stand in among the tracks and just look at the vast expanse of the railway lines is a staggering experience; to think that we had to learn this lot even more intimately than the palms of our own hands. This was undoubtedly the hardest part of our road learning campaign and took us nearly three weeks. We stumbled and clambered through countless sidings, watching signals and reading the roads to which they gave indication. Trains coming in and going out were closely watched and we observed the source of their respective instructions, whether from signals or pointsmen. When we had learned the different movements, such as wrong roads and shunting movements, the use of arrival roads and departure roads and all the associated procedures, we reckoned that we were reasonably conversant with the district, and were confident that when we took over as drivers and returned we should know what we were doing.

The next stage after Willesden was the last section of track into Euston Station. This was not very difficult, except for the empty coach line which runs under the main line and which starts at the south end of Primrose Hill Tunnel. The line drops steeply under the main line at Camden and rises just as sharply to make its exit at the carriage sidings.

On the original London and Birmingham Railway, Primrose Hill was the first high ground bored, and the stiff London clay swelling or contracting according to the weather at the time, made this a matter of no slight difficulty. The pressure of the wet clay squeezed the mortar through the the brickwork joints, causing the brickwork to fly off in small particles. The Stephensons, George and Robert, who were the appointed engineers for the line, were very mindful of the cave-in to the Preston Brook Tunnel on the Grand Junction Railway. To overcome the difficulty, Robert used only the hardest possible bricks, laid with Roman cement instead of mortar. The 845 yards long tunnel was constructed throughout in this manner, the brickwork being formed into a sound arch some 27 inches in thickness.

At the time of its construction there was a die-hard belief, sustained at both Parliamentary and public levels, that tunnels were unhealthy in the highest degree. Medical practitioners also shared this prejudice, but in 1837 two medical men, two surveyors, and a lecturer in chemistry inspected the Primrose Hill Tunnel. Their verdict was an unqualified vindication of the use of tunnels on railway constructions. They said, " . . . the air for many feet above our heads remained clear and apparantly unaffected by steam or effluvia of any kind." Their further opinion declared that the risks involved in travelling through tunnels were "no greater than those incurred in ordinary travelling upon an open railway or upon a turn-pike road." The fears that tunnels would prove to be detrimental to the health and convenience of the passengers were stated to be "perfectly futile and groundless."

But it is not health hazards that have made railwaymen give Primrose Hill Tunnel the nickname "Rat Hole", and treat it with respect. Many an engine man using the Tunnel, has, by being over cautious, learnt its secret the hard and humiliating way. The successful way of traversing this stretch of line was to wait for the repeater signal to show 'Clear' at the entrance to the Tunnel; then, instead of attempting to drive the loco and train through the canny driver allowed the train to push him. By this means, a speed of 40 miles per hour was quite easily reached, and believe me, the temptation to brake became very strong but the impetus of the 'controlled runaway' gave the necessary boost to lift the train up the sharp rise. If a driver succumbed to using the brake, he lived to regret it; because of the severe rise at the exit his train came to a state of rest, and the assistance of another locomotive was required.

After all this came London (Euston) Station. Here there is a veritable network of railway lines, a complex, which surprisingly, was not difficult to learn. All in all, it took about seven weeks to learn the road from Crewe to London and return. Along with the two other members of the 'Triple Alliance' I accomplished my learning programme, and reported back to the foreman's office at Crewe. I signed for the road on my route card and waited for my first job in London, but after all the effort of the last seven weeks I now wondered when this was to be.

Chapter VII
IN AND OUT OF THE SMOKE

As events turned out, I had only to wait a fortnight, but in my excitement and the hungry urge to get to grips with the job the time seemed to pass like a million years. During this eternity I was kept busy on various shunting jobs, and when I was not doing these I set about familiarising myself with my new depot. This of course entailed learning the names of various people and their relative status, together with procedures, methods, places, and the thousand and one things which make an organisation run smoothly.

One morning, after reporting in for duty, I read the roster sheet and discovered to my delight that I was detailed to work the 3.52p.m. from Crewe to London, this being the 1.40p.m. out from Holyhead. This was great stuff now I could put into practice the lessons I hoped I had learned during those seven weeks.

For this first working trip to London my engine was a Royal Scot Class 7P No. 46170, named 'British Legion', she being the first of her class to be fitted with a tapered boiler. She had been rebuilt in 1935 from the high pressure locomotive 6399, named 'Fury'. This latter engine had been built in 1929 on similar lines to, and a virtual modification of, the 'Royal Scot' class, and was introduced by the L.M.S. for high pressure trials, having a pressure rating of 1,400 to 1,800 lbs per sq. in. She was eventually withdrawn from service after tests and in later years came to grief by exploding.

After preparation at the Crewe North shed, my fireman, Terry Norbury, and I took our steed out to the station to await the arrival of the Holyhead train. This duty ran into Crewe dead on time, the Holyhead engine was hooked off, and she was trundled down to the North shed for servicing prior to the return home.

We backed up to the train, and while Terry attended to the couplings and brake connections I checked over the train details with the guard. He gave me particulars of the weight and composition of the train and checked the stops with me; on this particular run I had only the one at Rugby before Euston. With this essential formality completed we were ready for the 'off'. The guard, back on his 'home' territory at the rear of the train, gave us the green flag, waving it with a very smart 'wristy' action.

Then, with a quick checking glance at the signal at the end of No. 4 platform to make sure it gave the 'clear' away we went.

We had only nine coaches on, weighing some three hundred and twenty-four tons, so we were soon under way past the 20m.p.h. restriction. As we left the station behind I shortened the cut-off to a minimum and opened the regulator wide, then lengthened the cut-off to the cylinders until I was getting a healthy bark from the exhaust chimney. Basford Hall Junction was passed at 50 miles per hour, and we maintained this speed to Whitmore and over the top of the bank, before then topping up the water-tank on the troughs. As we were fresh out of Crewe with four thousand gallons we only needed roughly one thousand gallons to give us a full tank again.

We increased speed to well up in the 70's and were going like a 'bomb', when I turned to my young fireman and said, "Terry, this is my first driving job to London". He raised his eyebrows, and regarded me with a quizzical smile before answering. "I've got news for you Bert. This is my first firing job to London." We both roared with laughter, although, take it from me, we were both more than a little apprehensive about the outcome of the proceedings.

"Never mind", I said, "Just tell me if she doesn't hold her own". By this I meant that if the loco started to drop in steam pressure, or if there was any noticeable decrease in the water level in the boiler, I wanted to know about it. I would, of course, have known about any adverse circumstances as soon as he, but the comment showed him that I looked to him for help, and established us as a team.

I closed the regulator to coast round Norton Bridge at about 60 miles per hour, this being necessary because of the curves. With these safely negotiated I opened the regulator once more to roar through Stafford Station and junction. I glanced at my watch quickly and was pleased to note that we were bang on time. Through Milford and Brocton, into Shugborough Tunnel at full chat, and out at the other end, erupting into daylight amid clouds of steam and smoke. Over and above the noise of our passage Terry sang his head off—always a good sign that all is well with the fireman.

Passing Colwich signal-box I exchanged greetings with the signal-man, the wave of my hand and the short 'toot' on the whistle probably helping to relieve the monotony of his somewhat lonely day. Incidentally, the very handsome church here provides the last resting place of Lord Anson, the famous English admiral and circumnavigator of the globe, born at Shugborough in 1697 and buried in 1762.

We were up in the 90's now, and the loco was as steady as a rock, running effortlessly just like a sewing machine, and easing down towards Lichfield. But here we got our first signal check. The distant signal for Lichfield was on, so I closed the regulator rapidly. At the same time I slammed the brake on hard, feeling the bite through the wheels to the rails. Our speed decreased rapidly, so I eased the brake and came to a smooth stand at the foot of the offending home signal.

The instant we came to a halt my mate climbed down off the footplate to go to the signal box in order to carry out Rule 55. This is a protection rule for both the signalman and train crew. Its provisions require that the fireman enters his name in the signalman's train book; he is also required to list the time of his arrival at the signal, together with a reference to the appropriate line upon which the train is standing. In turn, the signalman countersigns the entries, and puts a locking clip on the signal lever, thus

46170 'British Legion' at Crewe Station on 22nd September, 1961.

(Norman Preedy)

ensuring that full protection has been made and that no other train can enter our section and run into us from behind.

The Lichfield signalman informed us that there was a parcel train in front of us, and that we would have to wait until this train was clear of the main line at Tamworth. This wait cost us about seven or eight minutes, and with such a tight-scheduled train as ours this meant that once we were under way again we should have to move a little faster.

Eventually we received the 'All Clear', and were away. Our aim was then to recover some, if not all, of that lost time, and in this endeavour I received full support from Terry. He fired the 'Scot' with enthusiasm and vigour and I commenced to drive her hard. Onward over the troughs at Hademoor, which are not guaranteed to top-up the tank, although we picked up about one thousand five hundred gallons. Through Tamworth at 70 miles per hour, with its handsome building, and then really belting along as we approached Polesworth. Going through the station we hit a bad piece of rail and the engine began to roll and pitch rather violently. I started corrective controls, at the same time stealing a sidelong glance at Terry who was looking a little perturbed at the loco's antics. I was about to re-assure him when we ran onto smooth track again. It was one of those situations where words could do nothing and yet, paradoxically, they were helpful. "Never mind Terry, we are over it now."

"Yes", he replied, "but it was a bit rough." He wiped his brow.

The anxiety was over, but believe me, it was a trying experience, being the first of many similar ones repeated quite often in my later years on various tracks up and down the country. The incident was reported in my log so that the track maintenance crew could attend to the faulty piece of track and so prevent a possible accident.

But the track still stretched ahead, and soon we both settled down to the task of recovering lost time. We flashed through Nuneaton at 85 miles per hour, and on checking my watch I was pleased to find that we had recovered a minute and a half—not bad at all for a couple of newcomers to the road. There then came another fast stretch approaching Rugby, and the stations at Bulkington, Shilton, and Brinklow blurred past. The engine was in good condition and I lengthened the cut-off another turn of the wheel. She responded immediately and soon we were back in the 90's, the exhaust a continual roar.

Newbold loomed up fast and the scoop was lowered as we flew over the troughs. We managed to pick up two thousand gallons but this did not fill the tank. There was no problem however, because we would be stopping at Rugby and could utilise the water column at the end of the platform. Indeed, as soon as we rolled to a halt at Rugby my mate leapt from the footplate and put the water column bag into the tender. I turned on the tap—after all, someone had to attend to the technical matters!

In the meantime the platform staff busily carried out their respective duties, such as emptying the parcels van and re-stocking it, helping the Post Office men with the mail-bags, looking after the passengers—"Is this the train for....?", "Where do I catch the....?" etc. Then the Departure Officer, watch and whistle in hand, made sure, along with the guard, that all doors were fastened properly. By then we had filled the tank and done our chores, so we climbed back on board 46170 and found time for a lid of tea and a Woodbine as we waited the signal to go.

Suddenly there was such a cacophony of whistles as the Departure Officer and the guard, each blowing his own tune, seemed to be trying to outdo the other. I thought for a moment, as I took a last puff at my cigarette, that we were at a football referees' convention gone berserk! But it was merely the signal for us to go, so with an answering blow from my own whistle that outdid the pair of them we went on our way again. Here I must add that due to our fast run between Nuneaton and Rugby we had recovered two and a half minutes; so barring any adverse signals and the minimum of permanent way restrictions we would not be too far out of time at London.

We left Rugby and headed up the slight incline to Kilsby Tunnel doing about 55 miles per hour. With a banshee shriek of the whistle we entered the black gaping mouth of the tunnel. The coughing of our exhaust crackled off the walls and roof in almost solid lumps of sound. About a quarter of the way in, 46170 took it upon herself to slip. A shower of red-hot sparks cascaded onto the roof of the cab, treating us to a firework display of gigantic and alarming proportions. This fifth of November exhibition was the source of much amusement to my mate, amusement which was short-lived when he opened the fire-hole door. He observed the detrimental results of the loco's slipping, finding that the fire had been shaken all over the fire-box. Gaping holes were left in the bed where the fire had literally gone up in smoke and up the exhaust as well—hence the shower of sparks. All this meant extra work for Terry, who, much to his annoyance, had to set about re-building the fire. With some quiet, and some not-so-quiet mutterings, he proceeded to do so.

By this time the 'Scottie' had decided to regain her lady-like composure, perhaps persuaded a little by my application of the sanders. However, just before we reached the other end of the tunnel our ear-drums were just about shattered by another express passing us on the opposite line, doing about 90 miles per hour. It is at moments like these that Time, for a fraction of a second, seems to stand still. One can see the other train approaching, and for a fragment of that fraction of a second there is the thought, the doubt, that there is going to be a God Almighty collision. Then with a sudden bark of exhaust the other engine is gone, sucking all the smoke with her. 'Thrum, thrum, thrum', the coaches whizz past, and the train is but a memory as the light at the end of the tunnel appears.

We rushed out of the tunnel and roared towards Welton where the M1 motorway on the left runs parallel to the railway. By now we were running at 75 miles per hour and the cars were streaking away from us as if we were stopped. Of course, in those days there was no 70 restriction on the motorway.

As we approached Weedon I closed the regulator and gently applied the brakes so that we could negotiate the curves and ease through the 60 miles per hour restriction. Instantly, my mate whipped on the live steam injector to take advantage of the chance to fill the boiler up to the maximum level. This was successfully done while we coasted round the curves, then once again the regulator was opened wide and the 'Scottie' went belting through Stowe Hill Tunnel. By this time coal dust was beginning to swirl around the footplate, so my mate wasted no time in remedying this nuisance. The slaking pipe was swung into action and water swilled onto the footplate; the pile of coal in the tender also had a shower-bath in an attempt to minimise the dust.

On through Bilsworth to Roade Junction, where we joined up with the line from Northampton. From here to Euston there is a double road with 'Up Fast' and 'Up Slow' lines plus water troughs at Castlethorpe. These were always good and we had no trouble at all in filling the tank. We fairly flew along with our speed in the 90's. To say that this was exhilarating is the understatement of all time. I have always enjoyed the tremendous thrill of going fast, with the extra bite of knowing that one is in control, knowing exactly what one is doing and the right time to do it. I consider that anyone who has missed the experience of a footplate ride at high speed has lost something wonderful from their lives. They have my commiserations.

It was necessary to coast around the curves at Wolverton, so on passing the Carriage Works to the right the regulator was closed and our speed dropped to the regulation 80 miles per hour. Then once safely out of the restriction zone—these curves are deceptively tight at speed—the regulator was opened and we roared up the slight incline to Bletchley. Over the top of the bank at Denbigh Hall and our speed was back up to 90 miles per hour, then through the blur of Bletchley Station with the brick yards on the right. A quick glance at my watch told me the satisfying news that we had regained four minutes from Rugby. I turned and informed my mate of this pleasant fact. His response blunt and to the point was accompanied by a cheeky grin which split his grimy face. "I should think so. You're going like a bloody madman, and I've got the sweat to prove it."

Our speed started to decrease as we passed Leighton Buzzard and started the climb to Tring. Cutting down to 55 m.p.h. 'British Legion' worked hard, doing everything that was asked of her. Terry sweated profusely but absolutely enjoyed every moment of his task. We reached the top of the bank just beyond Tring, then found ourselves under orders from a signal check, so steam was shut off to slow down, but as we approached the distant signal it changed to green. I could see no obstructions ahead so the offending signalman was 'blessed' for checking us.

I opened her wide again, and due to the falling gradient 46170 was back in her stride again, going like the proverbial 'bat out of hell', and heading through the 530 yard long Northchurch Tunnel at 80 miles per hour. Around the slight curve at Berkhamstead—where Geoffrey Chaucer the poet was clerk of the works at Berkhamsted Castle—and on through Bourne End, the scene of a tragic accident several years earlier. Our speed reached 90 miles per hour as we flashed through Boxmoor. Once again, as both Terry and I had frequently done since we started the run, I looked back along the train to see if everything was still normal. This was one of the laid down duties of driver and fireman, a necessary safety rule that soon becomes an almost instinctive action. All was well.

As we approached Kings Langley there was a permanent way speed restriction warning board posted by the trackside showing a restriction of 20 miles per hour. I immediately closed the regulator and applied the brakes, but driving more than 500 tons of locomotive and train at 90 miles per hour is somewhat like being in charge of the 'Irresistible Force', and having to come down to a crawling 20 in the space of one mile takes quite a bit of doing. I left the brakes hard on until they were really red hot. Our speed decreased appreciatively, and the smell of hot oil wafting by on wraiths of blue-black smoke was quite strong in our nostrils. By the time we passed the commencement of the speed restriction, indicated by a board with a black 'C' on a white background, we were down to the prescribed speed of 20 miles per hour. I breathed a sigh of relief. "I'll bet that took an inch or two off the top of the rails", laughed Terry.

The length of the restricted zone was somewhere in the region of half a mile, and our great expectations of arriving at London on time were dashed, now that the precious time we had recovered was being spent trundling along the restriction. Naturally enough, we had a few choice words to say to each other concerning the virtues of the permanent way gang working on the line and their parents marital status! All our efforts had been wasted, but this was one of the many frustrations that engine crews have to live with. Apparently this section of line had only just been relaid, and with no ballast between the sleepers this caused 46170 to pitch and roll a little. Held in check by the couplings, but individually upset by the uneven track, the coaches imitated the Scottie's rolling gait. Looking back along the train was like watching a drunken caterpillar out for a stroll. However, we eventually negotiated the restriction and I took careful observation to see that all of the train was safely past the termination board before opening the regulator.

I looked at my watch and was dismayed to find that we were right back to square one, exactly eight minutes late. I asked Terry what sort of fire he had on to which he replied "The biggest you've ever seen". "Right mate," I said, "I'm going to hammer this engine from here on".

I lengthened the valve travel and the bark from the exhaust increased to a continual roar as we prepared to enter the 1725 yard long Watford Tunnel. I anticipated the engine slipping and so applied the sanders. The wheels bit immediately and we kept going without trouble. Inside white hot sparks burst from the exhaust and ricocheted off the tunnel roof onto the cab, cascading in an off-white fury on either side of the footplate; the impression was very much like being in the middle of a fan of tracer bullets. Bursting out at the other end the sanders were closed, and we fairly flew as we passed the double junction and station at Watford. The enginemen here looked aghast as we thundered past, their gesticulations a criticism of my handling of the engine. It always looked more frightening to the bystander, so I suppose that I couldn't really blame them. I really drove her hard, thrashed rather than punished—but always kept her firmly in check.

We hit Bushey troughs at 80 miles per hour, before going over the top of the slight incline which leads through Harrow & Wealdstone Station, the scene of a tragic accident. We overtook a local suburban train on the electric line to the right of us, and then belted through Wembley, the twin towers of the Empire Stadium on our left, and on past Brent Junction. Travelling at 95 miles per hour we soon left the vast marshalling yards behind us, and approached Willesden where I knew the speed had to be 80. I eased the regulator and shortened the valve travel. My mate's gruelling task was over and he relaxed on his seat smoking a Woodbine. His begrimed face made him look as if he has just come up from a colliery. I, of course made a comment to that effect, to which he retorted that I didn't look so pretty either!

'British Legion' steamed majestically on through Kilburn, making a wonderful sight, I'll warrant. We entered Primrose Hill Tunnel at 55 miles per hour, then rounded the curves and out of the tunnel at 40, passing Camden shed on the right, down Camden bank, and into Euston Station. I noted the time—just five minutes late—which meant three minutes had been brought back from Watford. Terry and I look at each other and grinned.

When we came to a halt the passengers disembarked from the train, safe and sound, unaware of anything unusual about their journey. It's a funny thing about passengers, some people make a point of coming to the footplate to offer their thanks, others walk away totally oblivious of the fact that there is a locomotive up front anyway, while a few turn up their toffee-noses as though the crew were creatures from another planet. On this occasion, the guard added his compliments to those of the passengers—"Well done, chaps." This more than made up for those who ignored us.

Not long after our arrival a driver and fireman relieved us to take 46170 light engine to the Willesden sheds, there to be serviced for her return journey. Terry and I washed and had a good meal before making our way to the Crewe train and a journey home on the 'cushions'.

Back at my new home depot, I signed off duty and looked at the next day's roster to see what job I was on. I found to my delight that I was on another passenger, this time to Carlisle. It would be an understatement to say that I was elated; I just loved the northern run, and this would be my first Carlisle since coming to Crewe. However I still felt pretty good and well satisfied with myself after this first trip to London. I felt I had come a long way from those early days at Lostock Hall.

Chapter VIII
CARLISLE

Carlisle Citadel station with the southbound 'Royal Scot' (46226) and 'Thames-Clyde Express' (46113) on 25th February, 1958. *(Norman Preedy)*

Carlisle was an important traffic point in the days when seven railways converged on Citadel Station, and locomotives in black, red, blue, green and brown liveries could be seen at the various platforms. This importance was no less when, at the grouping of 1923, the number of railway companies using the station was reduced to two, namely the London, Midland & Scottish Railway and the London & North Eastern Railway. Despite later nationalisation and the formation of British Rail, Carlisle still keeps its importance, perhaps a little diminished; but it retains something that the legions of politicians and bureaucrats can never steal or vanquish—its 'romance' as the Gateway to Scotland.

On the day following my successful trip to London I booked in at 12.15p.m. to work the 1.45p.m. to Carlisle, stopping at Preston. The engine was a British Rail 'Patriot' Class 7P, number 45530, 'Sir Frank Ree'. I was making my usual pre-run preparations when the examining fitter came over to me. He inspected her condition and informed me that she was overdue for a mileage examination, but this did not mean that 45530 was in a dangerous state. I took little comfort from his words, especially as he went on to comment that the axle-box journals probably had a little excess play in them which might cause the engine to ride rough. I soon found out how true his prediction was.

We left Crewe on time and as we passed through Winsford at 70 miles per hour we were literally being knocked to pieces. As the big ends came round they kicked back with such force that my fireman and I were unable to sit down—we were lifted clean off our seats. So it was 'Standing Room Only' on 45530! But at least we were not as unlucky as the crew of a London & North Western engine in the early 1870's. Winsford used to be the principal centre of the manufactured salt industry in England. The salt springs caused subsidence of the land, and one day a steam engine and eight men were swallowed up, with scarcely a trace of the accident left save for a depression in the earth. I've heard of engine-men driving their locos into the ground, but that was ridiculous!

We emerged from the deep cutting beyond the old Hartford Junction, and roared over the top of the long embankment beyond Acton Grange and headed onto the famous Dutton Viaduct, which consists of twenty arches constructed from red sandstone. It is more than a quarter of a mile long and carries the line over the Vale of Dutton and the River Weaver. A few minutes later my mate was struggling to drop the water pick up as the handle was very difficult to turn, but eventually he managed to get it down as we sped over the troughs at Moore. We were on the last twenty yards but the float on the tender water gauge had not moved, which told us that we had not picked up a drop of water. At this stage of the journey the malfunction of the equipment was not serious since we had enough water to reach Preston.

I closed the regulator so that we could coast through Warrington, the home of the first newspaper published in Lancashire (the 'Advertiser', published in 1756). My mate turned the steam wheel of the exhaust injector on, to top up the boiler water level, but immediately there was trouble as the injector blew back. He whipped the wheel shut, but to no avail, as the injector still blew back. The top feed clack, which was situated on top of the boiler casing, had stuck; this meant that it would require an application of the time-honoured remedy to free it—that of course meant a sharp blow with the coal pick. Meanwhile, down beneath the footplate steps a jet of scalding steam was blowing out; this in turn lowered the boiler water level quite rapidly, so I had to make a decision to stop somewhere so that the matter could be rectified.

I decided to make an unofficial stop at Golborne Junction where there was a telephone at the signal. Meanwhile, the live steam injector was on and just held the boiler water level at half full, whilst the steam pressure dropped from 225 p.s.i. to 190 p.s.i. The situation was getting desperate

As soon as we rolled up to the signal my mate was off the footplate, armed with a coal pick to tap the offending water feed clack. He soon successfully 'persuaded' the clack to return to normal so I phoned the signalman to advise him of our delay. With five minutes lost by this mishap we re-commenced our journey. 'Sir Frank Ree' would have to pull his socks up to recover the lost time.

Bamfurlong Junction saw us speed through at 80 miles per hour, whilst Springs Branch locomotive shed soon followed on our right. I closed the regulator, to reduce speed through Wigan North Western station to the required limit of 50 miles per hour, then opened 45530 back up for the stiff climb that faced us. I really had no choice but to belt the engine, although the resultant knocks on the big ends were something tremendous indeed. My ribs became sore, as those of my fireman, through being banged against the side of the cab. This was turning out to be 'one hell of a trip'.

We climbed the bank to Coppull, then our speed increased as we descended the other side. Before long we were doing 85, so I closed the regulator, knowing that we would coast all the way to Preston Station. We hit Euxton Junction at 90 m.p.h., and 45530 rolled like a rudderless frigate in a heavy swell. There was a look of consternation on my mate's face, which didn't improve when he saw me grin down at him.

"It's nothing to laugh at, you mad fool," he stuttered.

I didn't help soothe his ruffled temper when I asked, "Have you ever been on a loco at this speed when she's gone over? It's alright as long as she rolls, and then rolls back again. But if she rolls, and rolls the same way again it's a case of 'Good-night nurse'!"

He started to swear at me, and for the next ten minutes I vow that he didn't use the same word twice. Such was the exquisite vocabulary of the

45530 'Sir Frank Ree' at Chorley on 5th September, 1959.　　　　　*(Norman Preedy)*

firemans' fraternity. Thankfully, it kept his mind from thinking too much about the rolling; it would not have improved matters if he had known that I too had been concerned.

We went slower as we passed through Farrington Curve Junction and by the time we passed Ribble Sidings we were down to 20 miles per hour for the run into Preston Station. We came to a halt right by the water column, so my mate jumped onto the back of the tender and put the water bag in, then I turned on the juice.

As I stood there, I looked down the train and saw a gang of loco men approaching. There was something determined about their walk. On reaching us the driver said, "We're relieving you and your mate. You have to give Preston Control a ring, as they have a job for you back to Crewe".

I informed him of the trouble we had had with the injector, and how rough the engine was. He didn't seem interested or concerned; all he said was, "Aye, she'll be alright." I later found out that 'Sir Frank Ree' had failed at Carnforth and that the driver had had to have a fresh engine.

This calamitous incident and relief in mid-journey, coming directly after my succesful trip to London, was most upsetting. I would have preferred to have stayed with my engine and sorted out her problems, but as events turned out, I suppose that I would have been no more successful than my relief driver. This was an unhappy occasion which robbed me of the chance of an express run to Carlisle. But that is no reason why I should rob you; if we cannot ride to Carlisle on the footplate, then let us, at least, do it together as passengers.

Lancaster Castle Station soon looms up after an uneventful ride from Preston. The castle, now a prison, is passed beyond the north end of the station and to the right, then we cross the River Lune by way of the Lune Viaduct, originally constructed of wood. A few miles further on, where the line diverts to Morecambe and Heysham, is Hest Bank, with the beautiful mountains of Westmoreland and Cumberland (now Cumbria) as a background. It is here that the west coast route comes closest to the sea. Riding in comfort as we are, it is difficult to imagine the difficulties which beset the railway constructors over the next stretch of track. Boulton-le-Sands had to be reclaimed from a peat moss bog more than twenty feet deep before the line could be laid whilst the cutting beyond the south end of Carnforth Station required the excavation of close on a quarter of a million cubic yards of earth, mostly limestone.

Continuing north, the line pursues its relentless way by climbing some two and a half miles of bank with a gradient of 1 in 134 before then plunging into the thirty feet deep Cinderbarrow Cutting. At the north end of this cutting we descend the bank with a gradient of 1 in 280, the only falling gradient for 'down' trains between Carnforth and Grayrigg. With more cuttings and embankments following the rails lead us into the former County of Westmoreland just as we pass Burton and Holme Station. One reason for the closure of this station was its distance from the village of

Holme, where flax-making was the principal industry. Also much of the limestone used for the construction of the line between Carnforth and Kendal was quarried at the nearby hill of Farleton Knott. Burton and Holme boasts four tracks, two running north and two running south with the two outer roads used for goods trains, thus enabling the passenger expresses to go their way without hindrance. A crossing of the River Beela soon brings us to Milnthorpe. This has the dubious claim to fame of once being the home of the Gatebeck Powder Mills, a gunpowder factory. After a succession of explosions and fatalities the works and its industrial railway were closed down not long after the Second World War.

The long hard climb to Grayrigg now starts with a vengeance, the line rising some 485 feet during the next thirteen miles, with an average gradient of 1 in 142. On our left we pass Hindcaster Junction where the old Furness Railway used to run, and just beyond the junction we travel over the old, now disused, Lancaster Canal. The Furness Railway, sometimes known as the Lakeland Railway, possessed the advantage of running through some of the finest and most picturesque scenery in England, being advertised by the Company as the 'Paradise of Tourists'. Beyond Sedgewick the gradient increases to 1 in 111 for one and a quarter miles, this being the steepest part of the bank south of Oxenholme. As we progress northwards by Hat Fell and Peat Lane we leave Kendal and its castle way over to our left then after passing under Laverock Bridge the line turns abruptly eastward towards Dockray Viaduct.

The tracks are the only things which appear to be speeding along; the surrounding mountains and hills seem to be with us for ever, moving so slowly in the background and yet matching us for speed. Then suddenly, we are lifted above all this grandeur as we cross the six-arched viaduct, three hundred and seventy feet long. Seventy-five feet below us is a tributary of the River Mint, which snakes into the Patton Hills to our left. The next landmark is Lambrigg Crossing, with a signal box we used to call the 'Lambrigg Dog Kennel' because it was so small; a little further on is the box at Moresdale Hall, which was about the same size.

Our engine crew would be working hard for the next two miles, coaxing the loco up the increasingly steep gradient of 1 in 106 before Grayrigg. this location has a loop line in both directions and until as recently as 1967 boasted a pair of ex London & North Western Railway signals. I wonder where they are now?

After Grayrigg the line starts to level out to Low Gill Junction and all around can be seen the old railway cottages with their unmistakable architecture. We pass through some of the most rugged scenery, so beautiful in its wildness, that you could ever wish to see. The Lune Gorge mountains rise for a thousand feet, and way over to the east the Howgills summitts in the Langdale Fell soar into the sky some two thousand feet above us.

The railway now skirts the Dillicar Hills, and the scenery around us increases in picturesque beauty and grandeur, the line passing through the great Dillicar cut. On a falling gradient the water troughs are passed over and we are able to see a breathtakingly memorable sight. An express train, travelling at about 85 miles per hour after flying down Shap, is coming towards us over the troughs. The fireman has lowered the scoop, and the instant it hits the water, wings seem to sprout from the speeding locomotive. As we pass this beautiful winged monster it is as if we were riding on an underwater railway, then, with a last damp caress from a water wisp, the strange 'bird' flies on past.

Dillicar Troughs sees Stanier 'Black Five' No. 44905 taking water during May, 1965. *(Norman Preedy)*

Once through Tebay, which used to be known as Loup's Fell (which is about 1½ miles to the west), the prospect of Shap Summit looms before us. The Shap bank is about four miles long with a gradient of 1 in 75, and runs through exposed, bleak and barren moorland. Halfway up the incline we pass Scoutgreen signal box, surely one of the loniliest outposts in England, with only the moorland sheep to keep the signal-man company. Just beyond, we pass through a cutting in the hard, rugged rock, which at 60 feet deep, is the largest cutting on the ascent. Then with Beck Head and Shap Lodge on either hand, we travel under an iron footbridge some 60 feet above the rails. The enginemen call this piece of iron lattice-work the 'Bridge of Sighs' the reason being that the railway starts to level out, and once past this bridge the fireman's work is done, and he is able to heave a well-earned sigh of relief. Believe me, I know the feeling!

Thanks to the efforts of the fireman and the skill of the driver we reach Shap Summit successfully. The highest point of the line is gained here, taking us to 1,000 feet above sea level, and 888 feet above the level of the line near Lancaster. It was from the granite quarries here that the stone used in the construction of the Thames Embankment was obtained, also the Shap Granite Company supplied stone for Southampton Docks and some of the surround to St. Paul's Cathedral.

Now our descent begins in earnest with the track taking us down through a gradient of 1 in 125 over the next eleven miles. On over the River Leith, a tributary of the beautiful River Eden, and through the glades of Thrimby Grange, passing both Lowther and Clifton. Lowther Castle, once the seat of the Earls of Lonsdale, is seen on the left, making a magnificent sight. Still on the falling gradient we pass through Eden Valley Junction, which served the South Durham & Lancashire Union Railway line to Kirby Stephen, which was closed in 1962. Once through the junction we run over the Lowther embankment and viaduct, the latter being constructed of locally quarried stone, and made with six arches, each of sixty feet span.

Before turning into Penrith we cross one of the Eamont bridges through to Eamont Junction. The station of the ancient town of Penrith is built close to the site of the castle, once the residence of King Richard III. Still northbound the railway runs through Inglewood Forest—not very many trees here to justify the name—and on to Plumpton with gradients falling to 1 in 169 and 1 in 184 with a few level stretches in between. Trains roaring down from Shap often reach very high speeds in the region of Calthwaite and Southwaite station, now of course, closed. Before reaching Wreay, the engine driver has to slow down to take the reverse curves. We then rattle over the rails on the Carlisle approaches, passing the once proud Upperby sheds on the right, and we glide into Citadel Station.

Carlisle Citadel Station is a rather interesting building on several accounts; its neo-Tudor style with dormer and oriel windows lacks only well-kept lawns and close-trimmed yews to create the impression of being the facade of a public school, with a castellated bell-tower and imposing archways leading to the cloisters. It is perhaps these entrance archways which contain the most piquant historical interest of all.

If you do more than glance above these arches you will see four carved stone plaques, two bearing heraldic devices, and two blank. The first two heraldic shields with encircling garters contain the armorial bearings of the Lancaster & Carlisle Railway and the Caledonian Railway. The two blank plaques are a memorial to industrial greed and distrust, so complex that several thousand words would be needed to tell the tale in full. However, to be brief—at a meeting of the Lancaster & Carlisle and the Maryport & Carlisle, held in September 1846, it was agreed to accept the tender from Messrs. John Stephenson & Co. to erect the station at a cost of £37,982, the cost to be defrayed among the four companies (Caledonian, L. & C., M. & C., and the Newcastle & Carlisle Railway). But agreement could not be reached on the proportion of costs, although these had been worked out according to the principles used in the newly formed Railway Clearing House, so several actions of law were undertaken to re-possess the land at Citadel belonging to the M. & C. Eventually this company elected a new Board of Directors, and a tenancy agreement was reached on April 2nd, 1851. The two blank plaques, intend for the Maryport & Carlisle and the Newcastle & Carlisle Railway's arms, now bear silent testimony to this historic squabble.

Chapter IX
THE TARTAN RUN

The days lengthened into weeks, job succeeded job, until I began to feel as much a part of Crewe depot as surely as if I had worked on the old London & North Western right from the start. I had long since been accepted into the crew(e)-mens fraternity but as the weeks lengthened into months I began to despair of ever learning the road to Glasgow. In the end, in desperation, and with no chances having come my way, I submitted a written application for the chance to learn. But it was to no avail—I was refused. Further applications followed, but always I was refused.

I felt very frustrated, and began to grow a chip on my shoulder as wide as the footplate; I hoped it didn't show. Then one day two vacancies occurred in the Glasgow cycle link. This was nothing to do with Scottish bicycle chains, but was a link staffed by extra drivers. From this reservoir of experienced footplate men could be obtained replacements in the event of a regular driver being unavailable for duty. In order of precedence there were two other drivers at Crewe who had to be approached before me. So with an eye to the future, and hoping to take up regular Glasgow work, I almost drove myself frantic praying that they would decline this invitation, thus leaving the field clear and enabling me to take advantage of a long-cherished wish. My hopes and prayers were eventually answered, the other two saying that they had no desire for this class of work, and so I was approached.

There was no need for my arm to be twisted in order to get me to say "yes", as I thought that I was better suited for the job anyway! Had either of those two chaps accepted they would have had to learn the road from Wigan (North Western) to Glasgow, their knowledge of the 'North Road' only extending from Crewe to Wigan; on the other hand I only needed to learn the road from Carlisle northwards. I also had considerable knowledge of the route via Blackburn and Hellifield to Carlisle and was thus well-equipped for any diversions that cropped up. These did so with considerable frequency, a state of affairs which proved a source of annoyance to me on several occasions for when one of these Carlisle jobs came up, and it was routed via Lostock Hall, Blackburn and Hellifield, it seemed that more often than not a driver who wanted a conductor-driver from Farington Junction would be given the job, when there were others, myself included, who had the full route knowledge. It seemed silly to me, and I never equated the economics of the situation with efficiency. I reckon that over the years it must have cost Crewe locomotive department untold thousands of pounds to secure conductors from other depots. When I used to have words with the shed boss, all he would say was words to the effect that I had a job to do, and should be doing it, not talking about other jobs.

Looking back, I suppose that this situation was only to be expected in an organisation of the public sector where the age-old contentious practice was carried on of promoting outside people into a specific job. In this particular instance, a foreman fitter to shed boss, rather than a practical engine-man with a thorough knowledge of engines, the different routes, and the other one thousand and one different problems which beset the loco man. Talk about putting sleepers where the rails ought to be.

My reaction to the approach made to me by the shed boss was one of excitement; me driving an express to Glasgow—what a thrill! But first I had to learn the road, and in September 1965 I was sent out to start this pleasant task.

The first leg of my journey was on the footplate of a 'Royal Scot' from Carlisle to Motherwell. 'Royal Scot' again. It seems as though my career was built around these splendid locomotives. Anyway, what else did I expect to find in the Border country—The 'Cornishman'? From Motherwell I joined the driver in the cab of a Glasgow suburban train, and on arrival at Glasgow Central he was kind enough to demonstrate to me the many station moves which I should have to perform. I feverishly wrote them down in the umpteenth edition of my notebook. These notebooks, which I compiled throughout my entire career had on more than one occasion proved to be an invaluable source of reference. I noted the size, type, position and operation of every signal and the section of line to which it referred; diagrams in profusion accompanied the notes.

For the next seven weeks I commuted between Carlisle and Glasgow, paying such attention to the road that, at any given time, I am sure that I could have counted the sleepers. This is not to say that I ignored my footplate companions—quite the reverse; nonetheless, part of my mind was detached from my awareness of them and I recorded the various items of information for future reference

On 6th November, 1965, I signed for the route on my route card upon arrival back at Crewe. Now I was qualified, by reason of my London experience, to work between London and Glasgow. I was within one step of achieving every express drivers' dream, and this made me extremely happy, but for every sugar coating there is always a bitter pill. It would be marvellous to be able to say that I worked this run by steam, but in fact, my first job to Glasgow was in the cab of a 2,750 h.p. Brush Sulzer Type 4, being the 4.15p.m. from Crewe (the 'Midday Scot'), but more of that later. I never had the opportunity of working the Tartan run on the footplate of a steam locomotive—more's the pity and my loss. But I did have one trip from Crewe to Perth with a steam engine, a 'Baby Scot', long before I had learned Glasgow. For this run I had to have a conductor driver from Carlisle to Perth and return.

However, before describing this run, I feel that the locomotive I used deserves a little mention. Several of the old London & North Western Railway's 'Claughtons' were rebuilt with large diameter boilers. These rebuilds appeared in several varieties, one of which, although having little left of the original engine in its re-construction, bore a marked resemblance to the 'Royal Scots'; it was immediately nicknamed "Baby Scot". The original four cylinders were replaced by three, and later 'Baby Scots' were brand new engines. For performance in relation to their size they had few, if any, rivals on the L.M.S., and their traction was only slightly inferior to the 'Royal Scots'.

Well, with such an engine I drove a football special train for an England v. Scotland International at Hampden Park. The rear eight coaches were uncoupled for working into Glasgow while we carried on to Perth with the front portion of the train, a rake of six coaches. On our arrival a passenger walked up the platform to us, and as he stood by the cabside, he reached into a pocket, held out his hand, and said, "That was a good run, driver. Have these as a token of my gratitude." With that he presented us, much to our surprise, with two tickets for the Glasgow match. Open mouthed and astonished, we thanked him, and he disappeared into the crowd; to this day I haven't the foggiest notion as to who he was.

Now our problem was how to get to the match from Perth. The conductor driver reckoned that there was no problem. "That's easily solved", he said. "You need a conductor driver back to Carlisle, don't you?" I agreed. "Well, if you ask the foreman at Perth shed to provide a fireman to Motherwell, you can arrange to be waiting there with your mate to relieve them".

So the whole arrangement depended upon the Perth foreman. Would he

L.M.S. 'Baby Scot' 4-6-0 No. 5512 'Bunsen' at Longsight shed, Manchester during August, 1935. (Norman Preedy collection)

be as co-operative as we hoped? I put the question to him, turning on the Stewart charm, till I reckoned I could have bewitched the hairs off a billiard ball. With all the solemnity of a judge he removed his blocker hard hat, and scratching his cranium, said, "Och, ah dunnaw." I started to explain the importance of the situation to him. "Aye, that's a verra weel. But what aboot yer sleep, mon?" Eagerly I explained that we could get some sleep on the train to Glasgow. I must have convinced him, for he said, "Well, ah'm nae one to spoil the enjoyment of a body. Fa mesel, it'll be a pleasure to see you Sassenachs beaten at futba."

So, with the generosity for which the Scots are famous, we were able to make satisfactory arrangements, and we saw the match at Hampden Park. Afterwards we made our way to the hostel in Glasgow, had a bath and a meal, and then went on to Motherwell. Our train was due in at 8.17p.m. and promptly to time it arrived. We climbed on board the same engine that we had had on the outward journey and as I took over from the fireman, I thanked him, and said, "Give our regards to your foreman at Perth, and tell him that I thank him for his consideration. Oh, and one other thing. Tell him that the Sassenachs pulverised the Scots to the tune of three to one." You can guess what his reply was!

As we pulled out of Motherwell I picked up the firing shovel and started to feed the fire, which I kept doing all the way to Carlisle while my mate gently eased her along. This enabled him to have a good rest, one that would stand him in good stead for the hard task that lay ahead—he would have to fire the engine from Carlisle to Crewe.

We ran into Carlisle Citadel a full two minutes early, giving us a vital bonus which we were able to put to good use by filling the water tank and bringing the coal forward in the tender. While we were doing this, we had the most pleasant surpise in the shape of a 'Black Five' backing on to us. The promise of assistance which this gave to us made my mate very happy; like myself, he was feeling extremely tired, as much I suppose, to the excitement of the football match we had watched as to our lack of sleep. However, we departed Carlisle on time, and the two engines fairly flew up the bank to Penrith. The fireman of the 'Black Five' must have been shovelling coal like an octopus for she was spewing a fountain of red-hot sparks so high in the air that my mate reckoned they were coming down coated with ice. I didn't see any myself, but I certainly agreed that the front crew were doing their stuff alright. On through Penrith and then we started to climb Shap, with everything feeling right, so I started to loose the 'Baby Scot' out.

As we shot over the top of the bank the signalman was leaning on the sill of his open window, one arm flung out with a exuberant 'thumbs up' gesture; we laughingly acknowledged with a well-known variation of the Churchill salute. Now both fireman could relax a little as we began to race down towards Tebay. Just a rub on the brake by the leading engine driver brought our speed down to 80 miles per hour as we powered through

Tebay, then over the troughs at Dillicar with the leading engine picking up water first, while we dropped the damper door and put the blower on hard in order to stop any blow-back from the fire. We had the last half of the troughs and filled the tank to within 500 gallons.

Onward we forged with a fast run down to Oxenholme, the lighted streets of Kendal away to our right, shimmering in the almost solid darkness of the night. The physical feeling that one experienced of the darkness in isolated places is difficult to describe to anyone except those who have likewise experienced it. In and around cities, towns and villages, the traveller by road is never very far away from the lights; even if the lights cannot be seen individually, their accumulative glow lightens the sky. But in some of the more deserted stretches of rail in Cumbria there was nothing save an occasional signal and the bright orange dazzle from the firebox to relieve the inky darkness.

Against the black back-drop of the Fells, and seemingly separated from us by an eternity of darkness, could be seen the slightly less black silhouette of the leading engine. The firehole glare shot a broad beam of orange light skywards from the cab, ricocheting as it hit the curved roof of the cab, leaving a flame-coloured fan in its wake. Coal dust and small pieces of coal beat continuously against our front windows, hammering and rattling like hailstones, and I could see the sharply outlined silhouette of the driver's head and shoulders as he concentrated on the road ahead. Every now and then he looked back at me to see that all was well.

We roared through Carnforth and passed two freight trains awaiting their turn on the main line, then over the Lune Bridge at Lancaster and up the short but stiff incline south of Lancaster Station, past the almost deserted Lancaster No. 1, and over the top of the bank. My mate came across the footplate, lurched would be a better description, and draped his arm across my shoulder. Slowly shaking his head, he said, "You know Bert, I'm dead tired". I looked at him over my shoulder, fixed him with a grin, and replied, "So what? Old soul, I've news for you. So am I". With that I abruptly turned back to my look-out position and scanned the way ahead, yet I felt the pangs of conscience at the unsympathetic treatment of my mate. I felt whacked, but deep down really knew how he felt also.

After about a couple of miles had skimmed beneath our wheels, I took out my fags, went over and offered him one. He refused me with thanks, saying that he didn't smoke;to which I suggested, "Will you have the money instead?" This brought a smile to his tired and grime-streaked face.

By then we were approaching Preston Station. I made the comment that we only had another fifty-eight miles to, go; this bit of information seemed to re-awaken him, giving a new lease of life to his tired body. On through Preston, up the bank to Coppull and over the top with both locomotives going like tornadoes, then after Wigan, we had our first signal check at Springs Branch. As we came to a halt I picked up the shovel and went into the tender to bring what little coal we had forward. My mate, armed with a coal pick, joined me. I half-turned, took the pick from him, and said, "Here, give me that. You go and sit down. I'll manage this little lot". The look of gratitude he gave me, you'd have thought I had given him the keys to the Bank of England; at any rate, I didn't need to tell him twice.

I had just finished raking, breaking, and stacking, and had put the tools away, when there came a long blast from the leading engine. Five minutes had elapsed since we stopped, and this was the signal that we were ready for the off again. I stepped back across the footplate just as we started to move, and my mate inspected the results of my labours. He nodded his appreciation of the stack of coal I had brought forward, saying, "When that lot has gone we shan't be far off Crewe".

We soon had the train rolling again at a fast pace and I started to sing some rock'n'roll number whilst stood in the middle of the footplate performing some weird and frantic gyrations which I fondly remember as the 'Twist'. Honestly, I don't think that I have ever felt less cheerful in my life than I did at that time; I could have dropped with fatigue but I didn't want my mate to see this. My antics seemed to have the desired effect for he picked up the shovel and threatened to crown me with it unless I shut up and sat down. This I promptly did, and he appeared to have forgotten his tiredness as, with some new-found energy, he started to fire. He continued in this manner until I closed the regulators for the last time on approaching Crewe. His huge sigh of relief was clearly audible across the cab but my own secret sigh escaped un-noticed.

Six minutes behind schedule we ran into Crewe Station. As we climbed from the cab, my weary fireman thanked me for the journey, and said, "If ever we go north together again and someone offers you some football tickets, please make sure that it's on our day off. I've never been so tired in all my life!".

Laughing, I patted his shoulder. "Well, you can go home now and spend the week-end in bed. I know I shall give my bed some hammer in a bit." We saluted each other with a "Cheerio, mate," and wended our separate ways home from the station, leaving just a few crumbs of coal littering the bottom of the tender.

Chapter X
FAREWELL TO STEAM . . . An Interlude

For some considerable time grim rumours had been circulating concerning the replacement of steam engines by diesels. We all knew what these things were, after all, they had been using them in the United States of America and various places on the Continent for years. But it couldn't happen here —or could it? Many enginemen, myself among them, argued that such a terrible thing could not come to pass, certainly not in our lifetime. But the writing was on the wall for the extermination, nay, brutal murder of the steam locomotive by British Rail.

With the withdrawal of steam locomotives on 11th August, 1968, came the realisation of a British Rail decision made in 1955; this realisation meant that one of the last bastions of the steam had tumbled to the diesel take-over. From the invention in 1893, generally accredited to Dr. Rudolf Diesel, of the engine which bears his name, to the application of this new type of engine to railway locomotion by the Swiss firm of Sulzer in 1912, and thence through various developments to the first English Electric 1 Co-Co 1 series introduced on British railways in 1958, can be seen the story of a world-wide take-over of traction in sixty-five years. It is interesting to note that the earliest regular use of diesels in Britain was on the 3 foot narrow gauge lines of the County Donegal Railways in 1930. The L.M.S. had a hand in the management of this Irish railway.

With the introduction of regular diesel services by British Railways there also emerged a new type of locoman; chaps who had not ventured beyond a fifty mile radius of Crewe with a steam locomotive were suddenly gifted with the courage to explore fresh fields and pastures new, and the story was much the same at all the other depots up and down the country.

The diesels are much cleaner and more comfortable to work on; there was no more exposure to the inclement weather, no more braving the elements in a storm-swept bleak countryside. There were no more worries about water levels and capacity, the problems of good and bad coal and shovelling it forward and stacking it. No longer was there need to wrestle with fire irons in front of a white-hot fire, watching the steam pressure drop alarmingly and fighting like mad to recover it. It now all belonged to the history books. These, and other similar instances, the very essence of what steam engine driving was all about, and achieved through countless generations of footplatemen, had come to naught.

The great satisfaction shared by the driver and fireman working as a team (only by their united efforts could a steam engine be persuaded to run successfully), of doing a good hard job together, was gone. Now the driving technique changed. With a diesel one simply climbed aboard, walked around the engine room looking for the more obvious defects, and when satisfied, started up the loco much the same as with a car. With the use of somewhat impersonal, unfeeling controls, the machine was backed up to the train that one was rostered to work, and then one sat awaiting the "right away" from the guard. As soon as this was given and acknowledged, the reverser was put into the forward position and—away we went.

Invariably, the fireman, or secondman, as he is now known, would lift his feet up and rest his weary limbs on the water pick-up or some other conveniently positioned piece of apparatus. He could be guaranteed to **remain in this position for miles on end until one was so inconsiderate as to** disturb him by asking for some tea to be made. It was not uncommon for a chap like this to go to London on a diesel and . . . But what sort of chap?, you might ask.

Well, every depot had one like him. For years and years he had had a bad back and as a result had done nothing but local shunt jobs. Suddenly, with the advent of the diesels, his aches and pains vanished like steam in the slipstream. He went to London, as I said, but found on arrival and to his dismay that the return job was being worked on a steam engine. All his miraculously cured ills suddenly returned a thousand-fold, so he reported sick and travelled home as a passenger. To be blunt, I, and hundreds more footplatemen like me would have sacked him on the spot and made him pay his own fare home. Fortunately for the railways, his kind were relatively few in number and were soon on the road to extinction; their worthy brothers were helping to carry on the traditions of the steam men and building new ones of their own.

I must confess that I held a very thinly disguised dislike for those men who usually had quite a lot to say about the job and its admitted short-comings. They were more vociferous than anyone else, and quick to recite to an audience the achievements of their railway careers and what they had gained, but never could one hear them tell of what they had put into the job. The truth of the matter was that they had done nothing, they were detractors and not constructors. I well remember one of these men holding the floor of the mess-room at Crewe North, telling the tale of his stirring exploits with the shovel between there and Glasgow, and what a good fireman he was. An old driver, one of the real old school, the breed for whom my boyhood adoration had grown into admiring respect, listened in silence while the tale unfolded, busily filling and lighting his pipe the while. As the story wound to its boring end, this driver fixed the conceited fireman with a baleful eye and said, "Fire a loco', you? You couldn't fire a cap pistol." This scornful riposte was delivered with the merciless precision of a fencing master avenging a sullied honour. The fireman's ego was well and truly deflated and he slunk out of the room amid howls of derisory laughter.

But grim rumours and bragging tales aside, like it or lump it, the diesels **were here to stay, and there was a job to be done, a railway to be run.** Perhaps even more important still, my wife and I had become accustomed to the habit of eating regularly! So, with a new challenge in my job, I agreed to train as a diesel engine driver.

In February, 1962, I passed the examination which enabled me to drive on British Rail's roads the English Electric Type '4' locomotive, rated at 2,000 horse-power. I quickly gained experience on other types as they were introduced (or as I was introduced to them), and on the 10th November, 1965, four days after signing for the route on my card, I had my first job to Glasgow. As I have previously mentioned, the engine was a Brush Sulzer Type '4'. This particular type of engine was a relatively new introduction, having first appeared three years earlier and has now become one of the most widely used main line locomotives operated by British Rail. Designed and built by the Brush Electrical Engineering Company at the Falcon Works, Loughborough, a total of 509 units were produced, each rated at 2,750 horse-power and weighing 117 tons.

On this first driving run all went well up to Carlisle, then we ran into a real pea souper with visibility down to zero, but fortunately I had the assistance of the Automatic Warning Signal (A.W.S.). Our 'road' from Carlisle was far from a level one, and undulated through a series of 1 in 200 gradients, varying in distance from 4 to 7 miles each, until the famous Beattock Bank was reached.

After a four mile climb through Beattock, the final assault was made on the summit by two short gradients of 1 in 75 and 1 in 80. As we cleared the Top, 1014 feet above sea level, the weather changed abruptly—it was just

The northbound 'Royal Scot' passes Shap Wells on 13th May, 1966 in the care of Brush type '4' D1848. *(Norman Preedy)*

like running out of a long dark tunnel into the bright light of day. The relief from tension in both engine and crew was markedly noticeable. We relaxed as we rode the switchback gradients for more than 20 miles to Carstairs, and from there followed the Clyde down to Glasgow. At this time there was a strictly enforced 75 miles per hour speed restriction in operation throughout the Scottish Region; we were careful not to let our engine's performance too closely match our own exuberance.

In 1964 more and more diesels were making their appearance, and the day was not far away when the positions of steam engines and diesels would be reversed, with steam locos becoming the unusual sight on the tracks. Electrification was also in progress on the West Coast line, so on the 1st May, 1964, I commenced training on the electric locomotives with a whole new technique of engine driving ahead of me. I learned of 'catenarys', of 'pantographs', of neutral sections of the overhead line where no power existed, and the circuit relations of seventy-six different fuses (if any one of them blew then the loco was rendered powerless). For the first week the words and phrases were a meaniningless jumble, but by the second week the haphazard mess of facts and figures began to assume some sort of order; it was beginning to sink in. My classmates and I were issued with reference books listing all the faults and failures we should be likely to encounter on the road. The third week of our training saw us on that road for some practical learning; now we would see how much of those previous two weeks of lectures had really sunk in!

Our travelling classroom was a spare electric loco from the new Electric Traction Depot, so one the drivers backed it up to a set of empty coaches standing in Crewe station. The instructor-driver, Frank Rowlands, supervised the coupling up and moved amongst us as we got the train ready for the road. When everything was to his satisfaction, he climbed up into the cab, calling out, "O.K., let's go."

I pressed the pantograph 'Up' button but nothing happened. Again I pressed it, hoping that this time the desired effect would take place—after all, we were in a locomotive, not in a fixture of the landscape. But I was unlucky with no response at all from the loco; not even one stone of ballast quivered from any unleashed power from the mighty engine. I looked round in consternation at the instructor, then to my mates, and back to the instructor. A puzzled group of trainee drivers then looked at each other, scratched their heads, and after much debating on the subject arrived at a conclusion. At this moment, impatient to be off in order that we could receive our practical lessons, Frank Rowlands turned to me and snarled, "Well, what's the matter with it? Let go." We eagerly told him that we suspected a blown fuse. With a look that clearly showed his resignation to a malevolent fate, he replied, "That's absolutely splendid, you thick-headed bunch of so and so's." (Or words to that effect!) "Get it replaced then." Obviously we had made the correct diagnosis of the trouble, so we replaced the faulty fuse and I once again pressed the button. Success. Contact was now made via the pantograph to the overhead line. We all waited expectantly for the main air pressure to build up to the required minimum of 75 p.s.i. before the exhauster button could be pressed and the brakes released on the train. As soon as the indicator came up to 75 I pressed the button and nothing happened. Oh no, not again. I could see myself being thrown out of training school on my ear.

We looked around at each other in bewilderment, but one genius among us had begun to 'twig' what was wrong, and looking like the proverbial cat that has swallowed the cream, he turned to the instructor and said, "Could it be a fuse?" Rowlands retorted "How the heck should I know? Go and have a look." This was done and the fellow returned to the cab and informed us that the fuse was in place, so it couldn't be that. He was asked if he had tested it, and with the answer being "No", back he went. Of course, the test revealed the fuse to be a dud. I am pleased to report that we did eventually become mobile!

We all learned one important lesson that day—Never take anything for granted. Look, and don't just wave your eyes around and hope that things are right. Make sure that they are.

We learnt later that while we were busy coupling up the engine, Frank had put her into fault condition by removing or altering some of the fuses. Of course, this was all unbeknown to us, as were not paying attention to what the instructor was doing at this stage, expecting our lessons to begin after we were under way. This was his way, and a successful one, of showing us the folly of taking a fuse for granted, the moral of the exercise being to check fuses and if they were in any way suspect—remove and test. By this similar trials and errors, plus good instruction, we were safely steered through our training period.

On 2nd July, we passed the examinations on rules and regulations concerning electric loco's and their driving technique, set for us by the Electric Traction Inspector and our own Footplate Inspector. Thanks to the first class instruction given to us by the long-suffering, and really very patient Frank Rowlands, we all passed with flying colours.

I should like here to make public my appreciation of the instructors, both of diesels and electrics, at Crewe; not only were they all excellent instructors, but their patience with the men made Job seem like an intolerant old man. Because of their thoroughness and the consequent inspiration they gave to the trainees, I believe that Crewe had less failures than any other depot on the London and Midland Region.

As with the diesels, the electrics were clean and comfortable, although the meaning of the latter word is limited to the driver's non-exposure to the weather and not to the manner of his riding.

The leather upholstered seat was very comfortable,—as long as the locomotive was stationary; but at the high speeds required to keep the expresses to a fairly tight schedule a driver was tossed about like a cork in heavy seas. It is hardly very civilised when an Englishman cannot have a cup of tea without the beverage being spilled in his lap. Opinions as to the cause of this unstable ride varied from criticisms of the suspension to the theory that the wheel arrangement /axle weight ratio was incorrect. But whatever the cause, on more than one occasion I have been thrown upwards and forwards out of my seat, thereby causing my foot to come off the emergency safety pedal. Believe me, on such occasions it was quite a mad scramble to regain normal driving position and composure.

I must hasten to add that only the British Rail Type AL 5 locomotive reacted in this way. The AL 6, the Metro-vics, and the English Electric types gave us a more or less smooth ride.

As the weeks passed by, more and more diesels and electrics made their appearance, arriving in a never ending stream. Instead of the steam engine being phased out of service gradually, it was withdrawn so rapidly that one could almost predict then the date of its ultimate demise. All types of steam locomotive, the beloved Iron Horse of countless generations of schoolboys, could be seen arriving at Crewe coupled three or four a time behind a diesel loco. Their destination was the scrap-yard at Barry in Glamorgan where they would sadly wait in line for their appointment with the breaker's acetylene torch. Such is the sad price that we have to pay for progress, and although I agree that we must never call a halt to genuine advancement, I feel that its payment could have been a little more humanely arranged.

On July 1st, 1967, my wife and I flew to Vancouver, British Columbia. As this was my first experience of flying I was somewhat nervous and more than a little apprehensive. I remember looking at the length of the massive **Boeing 707** and shaking my head in disbelief that it would ever get off the ground. I still think that if the Earth was not round it never would have succeeded. But as we climbed aboard, the chief steward hastened to re-assure me that all would be well. I could not share his optimism, but in the event he proved to be right.

Vancouver was a short stop-over on our route, so I did not have much opportunity to sample the local railway scene. We took our leave of this beautiful city and set out by Canadian Pacific Railway to Regina, about 1,000 rail miles eastwards, and the capital of Saskatchewan. With the C.P.R. being one of the best known railways outside of the British Isles perhaps it is worthy of a little mention.

This magnificent trans-continental line was born out of much political wrangling, and after agreements had been reached on a completion date of May, 1891, the Canadian Government offered a loan of £6 million to the Company. The condition attached to this generosity was the advancement of the completion date by five years. In order to complete the contract a minimum of 400 miles of track had to be laid per year. This called for some fast track laying, and in 1882 two miles per day was the average, but in the following year 3½ miles was the daily norm. On July 28th of that year a record was set which is not likely to be surpassed—6½ miles of track was laid, using up a total of 2120 rails weighing 604 ton! Finally, on November 7th, 1885, at a spike driving ceremony held in Craigellachie, the rails from the east and west were joined together, six months ahead of schedule.

We travelled in the 'Expo Limited' for which I had a diesel cab pass. This was put to good use when we arrived at Banff, more than 5,000 feet above sea level, and near to the railway summit through the Canadian Rockies. Being seated near the end of the twenty-two coach train, I had to sprint along the platform, aware of being the centre of attraction. Heads swivelled as I raced past seated passengers and standing spectators, who probably thought I had gone mad. Never before had I realised how immensely long twenty-two coaches and three diesels could be, so as I arrived at the leading diesel I was puffing and blowing like a grampus.

After a suitable period to recover my breath, I climbed aboard to be greeted by a beaming giant of a man, a sort of six feet four inches welcoming committee. He uncurled himself from his driving seat and introduced himself with a name that was most inappropriate to his dimensions. "I'm Robert Small, welcome aboard", he beamed. Also there was a footplate inspector, to keep a regulation but friendly check on me, and the baggage man who additionally performed the duties of second man. After handshakes all round, we were soon ready for off, so the baggage man retired back to the train to give me more room. As we left Banff I began to view the awe-inspiring mountain scenery, when suddenly my pleasure turned sour and I cursed.

"What's the matter, Mr. Stewart?" enquired Robert. I replied "In my excitement at being able to have a ride with you, I've left my cine camera back in the train."

"You sure aren't the first person to do that. It's happened before," said the engineer sympathetically, despite a big wide grin spreading across his granite-like face.

Accepting the wisdom of the old saying, 'It's no use crying over spilt milk' it was not long before I was again gazing with rapt amazement and wonder at the grandeur of the scenery through the panoramic windscreens of the giant diesel. The orange-red loco, with its two like-coloured bankers and silver coaches, snaked alongside the swirling, bright blue waters of the river which flowed just ten yards away from the railway. On either was side was an absolute sea of dark green foliage stretching for miles, quite the largest and densest forest I have ever seen. Beyond, but looking quite close, were the snow-capped mountain peaks.

For me, the most marvellous sight from the front end was the succession of cantilever-arched trestle bridges, their original timbered construction now replaced by iron girders. We would approach a chasm round a curve in the headland with nothing beyond us, or so it seemed, save a vast tree lined drop. Then as we continued, the line just went out into space, gently supported by the graceful arch of a deceptively frail looking bridge. Long after we had safely crossed the chasm I would look back at the curving silver caterpillar of the train, its rear coaches still in the process of coming up to the bridge, and wonder how such a delicate structure could carry the weight of such a heavy train.

One curve we negotiated was so tight and severe that the driver had to drop our speed to a mere 5 miles per hour. The track was almost a 'hairpin bend', and I commented that, even at our snail's pace, the tension on the draw bar must have been terrific. The driver and the inspector nodded in agreement, the latter saying that it was not uncommon for freight trains to break loose while taking this curve. Considering that the curve is on a single line with block post 'signal boxes' anything up to one hundred miles away in either direction, I shuddered to think of the necessary protection procedure. Not being familiar with the C.P.R. Traffic Operation routines, the enormity of the situation was beyond my comprehension. Granted that there is an abundant supply of telephones at the lineside specially placed for such an emergency, but what of the event if the wires were down? The thought did not bear further contemplation, so I turned back to the much more pleasant task of enjoying the view.

I was getting my fill of the most beautiful ride I have ever experienced, either before or since. For the next two hundred and fifty miles I bobbed about that diesel cab like I was treading barefoot over red-hot coals. First to one side and then to the other, eager not to miss a thing; I reckon that I was even more excited than I had ever been as a lad.

It was an extremely tired, though still tremendously excited Bert Stewart who climbed off the diesel at the end of this first-class 'guided' rail journey. I thanked and bade farewell to Robert Small, and retired to our berth in the rear coach.

Our arrival at Regina the next day was delayed by some three hours because of a derailment outside Calgary. My wife and I were met at the station by my cousins, and between us, we lived it up for the next eleven days. Afterwards we took a morning flight to Montreal and paid a visit to EXPO 67, before returning home from our 'Holiday of a Lifetime'.

Chapter XI
HEAVEN IS AN A4 FOOTPLATE

In the closing weeks of 1966, as I cycled along the approach road to Crewe South shed, I observed a strange looking engine standing on number six road, which aroused my curiousity. I had never before seen one like this. I booked on duty and asked the foreman from which planet the 'foreigner' had descended. He told me that it was an 'A4' from the old London & North Eastern Railway, which, of course, I really knew. He further explained that she was waiting to go into Crewe Locomotive Works for a major overhaul, having been bought by a private society who wished to run her hauling specials on British Rail tracks.

As I had a few moments to spare before commencing my duties I decided to have a closer look at this big stranger, so I walked along beside her and stood looking at the big driving wheels and the motion, thinking "This baby should move along at a rate of knots". The nameplate, fixed to the forward part of her boiler casing, read 'Sir Nigel Gresley'. Fascinated, I climbed onto footplate and looked around. What a dreadful sight, everything was covered in rust and soot. I was both annoyed and saddened that this lovely locomotive should have been allowed to get into such a frightful state. However time dictated that I should be on the way to Basford Hall to join my train, so I left the sleeping 'Knight' rest peacefully in pastures new.

Two days later saw me waiting to leave Carlisle with the 8.45 a.m. to Crewe. An elderly gentlemen came up to the cabside of the diesel and bid me "Good morning" before enquiring if I was the driver. I replied, "Yes", and we started to chat away about railways in general. In the course of our conversation he mentioned that he had had quite a lot of footplate experience between Carlisle and Leeds, but since he had done very little travelling in this way between Carlisle and Crewe he wondered if there was the chance of a ride this morning. I enquired if he possessed a footplate pass, and this he produced. My examination of it showed that it was all in order. "O.K.", I said, "Climb aboard."

Eventually I was given the signal to proceed, and as the engine pulled away from Carlisle my companion and I continued chatting about railway matters and the like. He then introduced himself as the President of the A4 Locomotive Society Limited, proud owners of the 'foreign' engine residing on my home depot. His revelations filled me with great interest, to say the very least, and we talked of the wonderful prospect and the tremendous potential involved in the preservation and ultimate running of this magnificent locomotive. I eargerly made it known to him that in the event of the engine being put into running 'nick' and specials going from Crewe, I hoped he would be kind enough to consider me for the job as the driver. His reply to my hopeful request gave a little insight into the image of British Rail held by the lay public at the time. He said that he thought all present-day engine-men were more concerned with diesels, and when the day dawned that 'Sir Nigel Gresley' was restored to her former glory, he imagined that the driver and fireman would have to be press-ganged to work her.

I hastened to set him right. A real, live engine-man having to be dragged to the footplate of such a masterpiece of locomotive engineering? Not likely, having to be dragged away, more like. "There'll be no need for press-gangs, no shortage of volunteers. In fact, you've got a ready made volunteer here already", I said. "I'll do my utmost to drive for you."

He thanked me for my undoubted interest which so obviously pleased him, but expressed the opinion that it would really be up to the shed boss to pick the crew. Somewhat sadly and reluctantly, I had to agree with him.

As we neared Crewe, and while dreams and schemes whirled through my mind, I asked for another look at his footplate pass for I had forgotten his name. He willingly produced the document, and this time I made a firm mental note of the name—Sir Gerald Ley. From that day onwards we have been firm friends. Destiny or just plain co-incidence, call it what you will, that chance meeting with Sir Gerald was to add an extra dimension and fulfilment to my life as an engine driver.

This strange locomotive which I had first seen on the approaches to Crewe South shed is, by any standards, both unusual and famous; I think that the 'family roots' deserve further comment.

On March 5th, 1935, a standard A3 Class Super-Pacific made an experimental run from London to Newcastle. The locomotive, named 'Papyrus', was used by the London & North Eastern Railway to test the feasibility of running a regular ultra-high-speed train service in Great Britain. She attained the astonishingly high average speed of 80 miles per hour over 300 miles of track, and also gained a world speed record for steam locomotives when she touched a speed of 108 miles per hour on the descent of the bank from Stoke Summit to Peterborough.

Because of the success of this experimental run it was decided to design a modification of the A3 Pacifics. This new class of locomotive was to make the fullest possible use of stream-lining techniques, and in order to achieve the maximum efficiency for the new project, the train was made an integral part of the design; all projections on exterior surfaces of the coaches were removed or minimised, and the gaps between coach-ends closed.

The new Class A4 4-6-2 locomotive was born, having been designed by Mr (later Sir) Nigel Gresley, 2509 'Silver Link' was the first built, and weighed in at 165 ton in working order. By far the most dramatic feature of its design was the streamlined shape, with the top level of the boiler joined to the buffer beam by a beautifully curved casing which continued over the wedge-fronted cab roof, ending in a flexible connection to the top of the tender, thereby completely enclosing the crew. Removable valances covered the wheels, and were joined to a running board which swept back to the cab in a gentle curve somewhat similar to an aerofoil section.

94

For this special train the standard green livery of the L.N.E.R. was abandoned in favour of a very distinctive three-tone grey. The normal varnished teak of the coaches, for which the Company was famous, was similarly abandoned, so that with chromium fittings replacing brasswork, a most striking effect was achieved. The seven coaches, which were articulated, included a three car restaurant set with a kitchen in the centre. The total seating accommodation, including the restaurant car, was for 198 passengers.

Three days before the inaugural run on September 30th, 1935, the 'Silver Jubilee' express hauled by 'Silver Link', and driven by J. Taylor and fired by A. Luty, set out from Kings Cross Station on an experimental run. On the outward to Grantham four world's records were created, the train twice attaining a maximum speed of 112½ miles per hour near Arlesey and then between Biggleswade and Sandy. Of course, three years later sister locomotive 'Mallard' attained the world speed record for steam traction of 126 miles per hour near Essendine. A bronze plaque is fixed to the boiler casing of this locomotive recording the event, which is now likely to stand as an all time record.

Early in the spring of 1967, 'Sir Nigel Gresley' trundled out into the daylight from the Crewe sheds. She was resplendent in her newly painted blue and black livery, and made a most impressive sight. She was beautiful. The many thousands of pounds which had been spent on her complete rebuild was money well, and lovingly, spent.

I went to see the shed boss to enquire of her future running on British Rail tracks. He informed me that plans had been been made for her inaugural run on the 1s April, 1967, this being from Crewe to Carlisle direct but returning by way of Hellifield. I immediately made an official request for permission to drive 4498 on this occasion and to bolster my request I pointed out that I was fully conversant with the round trip routes. Quite naturally, the boss wanted to know what experience I had of this class of locomotive, to which I could only answer, albeit regretfully, "None whatsoever". The shed boss naturally gave a non-committal reply, "Well, we shall have to wait and see."

My great expectations began to decline, and I could see my dreams and schemes tumbling around me. But I had fallen in love with that locomotive and I was determined that my devotion would not go unfulfilled. I rang my new friend, Sir Gerald Ley, at his home. After listening to my account of the conversation with the shed boss, he advised that I get in touch with the secretary of the A4 Society, Philip Heald, at York. I did this without delay, stating in my letter the reasons for wanting this 'dream of heaven' job. By return of post came a most charming letter thanking me for my eager interest, and saying that my name would be recommended to the Divisional Superintendent at Stoke. I sat back and waited, impatiently I might add, for my destiny.

At about this time, our shed boss was due for retirement and his replacement was taking over. I went across to his office one day to enquire if anything further had been done concerning my request. After listening patiently to my impatient enquiry, the gentleman, for such he was, showed me a letter from the Divisional Superintendant. I could hardly believe my eyes, but there it was, in black and white—instructions that I, Herbert Banks Stewart, was to be the driver of 'Sir Nigel Gresley' on 1st April. I choked out my thanks to him, not forgetting the Divisional Super, and somehow made my exit from the office. I felt as if I were walking on air—nay, floating on a cloud of steam!

In the middle of March, I was informed that 4498 was to be hooked up to a parcels train for running in and testing, I would be installed as driver for the week in order to familiarise myself with the controls, which were somewhat different to the ones I was used to, but there's only one way to get to know a locomotive.

The train was the 11.45 pm from Crewe to Preston stopping at Warrington and Wigan. I booked on for duty at 11.05 pm and found that the engine had been fully prepared for my fireman and myself; there was nothing to do except climb aboard, deposit my personal effects in the locker, and get accustomed to the controls. The brake, as I found and half expected, was the simple vacuum type, but the regulator was the pull-out type as opposed to the more usual and familiar lift variety. The regulator quadrant was situated under the manifold and high over the firebox door. The latter opened with a double swinging action as opposed to the usual type mounted in grooves for easy access. The fire-hole door has a flap in the middle through which one can fire; this is a most important asset which enables the fireman to keep out the cold air.

As I moved around the cab eyeing things up and down, and generally getting the feel of things, our new shed boss and another young man came aboard. It was during the course of introductions that I learned for the first time the name of my new gaffer, Mr. Dentith. He introduced the A4 Society's secretary, Mr. Heald, with whom I had been corresponding; I was delighted to meet him, and thanked him for his efforts on my behalf. The shed boss asked if there were any problems, to which I replied that there were none as yet, indeed, as far as I could see, everything was ship-shape and Bristol fashion.

"Good. Glad to hear it," said Mr. Dentith, "because Mr. Heald will be riding with you to Preston and back to Crewe."

"O.K. Glad to have him with us," I replied.

At 11.25 we went off the South Shed to back onto our train in the Down yard at Crewe Station. As we approached the signal which controlled this yard I gave I gave a blast on the chime whistle. For a moment I felt like the Master Puppeteer in Toyland, for regardless of what they were doing, everyone swivelled their heads in the direction of this pleasant but unfamiliar sound. As soon as we had backed up to the train we were surrounded by a multitude of railwaymen and others, casting their eyes over this beautiful, former crack express engine of the L.N.E.R. I am sure that if they could have done so, they would have picked us up and carried us shoulder high. I was immensely proud that I was in charge, and I bubbled and trembled with such emotion that I cannot possibly describe. It was as if I had never been on a steam engine before. It was an absolutely glorious feeling. But for every 'Magic Moment' there has to be one of Reality. Amid all this hullabaloo and excitement, and seemingly unaffected by the fact that we had one of Sir Nigel Gresley's famous locomotives at the head of the train, indeed the very one which bore his name, along came the guard. Very matter of fact, he informed me of the composition of the train, and instructed that since there were some short wheel-based wagons included our speed limit would have to be 45 miles per hour. Immediately, the steam-struck schoolboy in me disappeared and the experienced engineman took his place, ready for the off.

The crowd, as if obeying a cue, stood back. Away we then went, over Crewe North Junction at 20 miles per hour, and then I gave her a little more steam; in no time at all we were doing the regulation 45. She was running perfectly, so sweetly. Both Philip Heald and myself were satisfied. Awaiting our arrival at Wigan were a few non-railway persons armed with cameras and flash-lights, just as there had been at Warrington. News certainly travelled fast. Philip and I speculated on how these enthusiasts obtained their information and decided that their sources were far and wide, strategically placed; probably friends in various railway offices who passed the word along.

Our journey onto Preston had all the signalmen hanging out of their windows, excitedly waving as we whispered by; having to keep her down to 45 meant that we were almost on silent running. Our arrival at Preston caused little short of turmoil. Everyone, or so it seemed, was there to greet us. Railway personnel, Post Office workers, Control room staff and others milled around, jostling to see this big stranger in their midst. All admiring, all full of questions. Who? What? Why? When? What is she doing on this train? To whom does she belong? What are the future plans for her? Shall we be seeing more of her? and so on. But Philip Heald took it all calmly in his stride, answering the excited questions as if he were holding a pre-arranged Press conference.

Eventually we were able to unhook our train and turn 4498 round for the return journey to Crewe, hauling the 5.45 a.m. stopping train calling at all stations. The empty coaches were situated in Dock Street Carriage Sidings, and consisted of six vehicles weighing in at 198 tons. After the coupling up prodedure was finished I went along to inspect the outside motion of the gentle giant I had been driving. I slowly rubbed the back of my hand against the wheel bosses and side rods, and anything else that was likely to have a tendency to overheat. She was as cold as ice.

The examination finished, we drank a cup of tea and ate our sandwiches.

Our sandwiches? More like mine! I must also add that Phillip smoked my cigarettes with such gay and casual abandon that I could not see how he was going to fulfil his promise of buying me some later on. In any event, he never did. The cigarettes that he owes me from 1967 onwards, well I should have enough to set up my own tobacco business!

At 5.25 we drew the train out of the sidings and into the station, once again surrounded by railwaymen. Another barrage of questions hit us, which Philip answered and parried well. Then, promptly at 5.45 am the guard waved his flag and we were 'Right Away'. Now we should be able to see how free running she really is. Once over the Ribble bridge I opened the regulator a little wider; the response was immediate, and we were doing 60 miles per hour in no time at all. It was my intention to go fast in order to test the bearings and see if they would remain cool at the kind of speeds which 4498 was capable of doing. Mind you, for all the effort she needed we might just as well have been hauling a bag of feathers behind us, such was the ease of her performance. Between Preston and Wigan we reached a speed of 75 miles per hour quite comfortably, and on arriving there I had sufficient time to spare to test the bearings for any signs of overheating. She was still as cold as ice. This was re-assuring indeed, and I gave the 'thumbs up' sign to Philip, which brought a huge grin of satisfaction to his face.

At this stage I must place on record the sterling efforts of my fireman on that trip, John Elliott. Unlike myself, he had experience of this type of

'Sir Nigel Gresley' at the head of the 5.45 a.m. Preston—Crewe at Earlestown station on 23rd March, 1967.

(E.N. Bellas)

locomotive, having served a spell of duty during his career by working on the London & North Eastern, and his firing turns were obviously standing him in good stead. Quite a lot of initial worries were taken from my shoulders by John and his excellent firing. Many thanks, mate.

After Warrington we attained a speed of 80 miles per hour. The ride on the footplate at this kind of speed was quite unique; there was, every so often, the merest fraction of a roll, almost like being back in the cradle. It was absolutely splendid. On arrival at Crewe we were greeted by Mr. Dentith who, not unnaturally, enquired how 4498 had behaved. The report of my findings was full of praise for her, and needless to say, Philip Heald was equally highly delighted with the locomotive's performance. We had here a locomotive of exceptional qualities.

This proving run was repeated over a period of four days during the week. Technically there was little difference between these repeat runs, but in one other aspect there was a vast contrast to that initial trip. On that first night only a few people knew of 4498's duties, but by Wednesday it was quite a different story. On our arrival at the various stations we were greeted by half the population of Northern England, or so it seemed. Certainly the platforms were crowded more with railway enthusiasts than passengers. They really had a field day, their cameras and tape recorders working overtime. But on the Thursday and Friday of that week 4498 was taken off duty for a boiler washing out and a final examination by artisan staff prior to the inaugural run.

The firemen for this run were selected after consultations between Mr. Dentith and myself. Out choice fell upon two passed firemen, Neil Cadman and Richard Howarth, both extremely capable men with the shovel, and both with proven wide knowledge of engines, their operation and construction. On the last day of March, the three of us were invited to a little 'get-together' held by the directors of the A4 Society at a Crewe hotel. At this party I was introduced to Julian Riddick, Mr. Newton and Sir Gerald Ley, whom I had met previously. These three gentlemen were the very personification of engine drivers; I am sure that this is what they would have wished to become had circumstances been different. I was fascinated by their wide ranging railway knowledge, more than the average layman, and their conversation had a fluency only possible from people who have a certain knowledge of what they are talking about. It can sometimes be a little boring to hear other than engine men talking of valve travel, cylinder bore, and tractive effort. But not these chaps, who provided us with a most stimulating evening. By the time we bade them farewell the excitement was built up for the following day.

As I walked home that night I began to make plans for my schedule on the morrow. Back in the house I studied the list of timings until they were firmly fixed in my mind, and I read and re-read the fortnightly notices issued by British Rail, paying particular note to the speed restrictions. By this means I hoped to avoid the need for looking at the book while we were running. Eventually I went to bed just after 1.30 am and dropped immediately into a dreamless sleep.

When I awoke about 8 o'clock I was thoroughly refreshed and rarin' to go. Throughout breakfast I was more than usually silent, my head buzzing with thoughts. My wife was prompted to enquire if anything was wrong, but I re-assured her that I was thinking about the forthcoming events of the day, and hoping that I lived up to the confidence placed in me by Mr. Dentith. "Well, this is a fine time to start thinking like that", she said. Her words soon shook me out of my inward thinking, and I gathered up my gear and started out on the walk to the depot. "See you on the train", I called to her as I left. "Don't be late". Along with Mrs Cadman and Mrs Howarth, my wife had been invited by the A4 Society to travel on the inaugural run, and like them, was looking forward tremendously to the occasion.

My official booking-on time for the day's duty was 10.15 am but I presented myself fifteen minutes earlier so that I could settle the tension which was gripping at my insides. The way I felt, one would have been excused for thinking that this was my very first trip on a steam locomotive, however, as I booked on and read the special notices relating to the Carlisle road, I began to calm down. My colleagues in the drivers' lobby wished me the best of luck and a good trip. Of course, for any great moment, there always has to be a comic. That day being no exception a voice growled in my ear, "Mind she doesn't run away with you". I turned around ready to give someone a bunch of five's and found myself looking up at six feet two of Bill Norburn, grinning from ear to ear. Trying to look fierce, something quite impossible since I too was grinning now, I said, "It's a good job you are not three inches bigger or I would have floored you!" Thanks, Bill, you did a good settling job for me that morning.

When all the good-natured banter has subsided I gathered my gear together and walked across to platform no. 3. As I strode up the ramp at the end of the platform I had my first taste of what was to follow, for there were literally hundreds of people gathered to see this wonderful engine and to give her a good send-off. (The B.R.B. must have made a fortune with the sale of platform tickets that day). I pushed my way through the dense throng of people just in time to see 'Sir Nigel Gresley' come gliding into the station. What a magnificent sight. As she 'whispered' alongside the platform there was a spontaneous and sustained outbreak of tumultuous applause from the crowd, something I shall never forget as long as I live.

Eventually I arrived on the footplate to be greeted by the directors of the A4 Society. Resplendent in overalls and peaked cap were Sir Gerald Ley, Julian Riddick and Philip Heald and, lo and behold, there was my chief from Stoke-on-Trent, Mr. Robert (Bob) McMurdie, dressed the same. As he greeted me, I thought to myself that we should not go short of help in firing the 'Blue Lady' for Mr. McMurdie was well acquainted with Gresley Pacifics as he had been a fireman at King's Cross in the early days of his railway career.

I deposited my gear in the locker, and stood watching for a moment or so as my two fireman, Neil and Richard, built up the fire, expertly dodging the legs of the extra 'crew' as they swung the laden shovels. On looking out from both sides of the cab, you could see people everywhere whilst cameras of types clicked and whirled away.

Before long the guard came along through the tender corridor to pass on to me the composition of the train, which was twelve coaches totalling four hundred and twenty tons, giving four hundred and fifty tons loaded:— Carlisle next stop. At 10.45 he waved his green flag and we were away.

We left the station with the chime whistle working overtime, then once over the Crewe North Junction I pulled back the reverses and opened the regulator wide. There was a healthy bark from the exhaust as we climbed the slight incline to the canal bridge at Winsford Station, then on the falling gradient the other side we began to fly along at hurricane speed. Through Hartford Station at 82 miles per hour, and by this time the guests on board were visiting the footplate by means of the corridor tender. To those not accustomed to footplate rides the experience was both wonderful and terrific, indeed some of our visitors were scared stiff and yet highly delighted at the same time. At frequent intervals small crowds had gathered at the trackside, cheerily waving us on our way. Never before had I seen such keen interest shown by the public in the passage of a steam locomotive. It was incredible. We went over the top of the bank at Weaver Junction doing a steady 79 miles per hour. On through Preston Brook, and by the time we were approaching the first water troughs at Moor our speed was up to 92 miles per hour. Neil Cadman, who was taking the first spell with the shovel, now prepared to take on water.

My shed boss, Mr. Dentith, was acting as a guide to the passengers, escorting them from the train to the footplate, and I advised him of our rapid approach to the troughs. I thought it best that the passenger visits were curtailed until we were over and well clear of the water. Somehow my warning was misunderstood and just as Neil dropped the water scoop Mr. Dentith and Mrs. Riddick started to walk through the corridor of the tender. The results proved calamitious for them. Because of our speed the water poured into the tank at a furious rate with the consequence that the turbulent water cascaded over into the corridor saturating them both. Mrs. Riddick's beautiful coiffure was ruined, and she left the tender in bedraggled fury, and understandably so; fortunately, the incident later became a source of amusement for her.

Our allowance for the twenty-four miles between Crewe and Warrington was twenty-five minutes; it took us just twenty-one minutes fifty-nine seconds, but then we encountered our first permanent way speed restriction—40 miles per hour at Winwick Junction. Once clear of this, however, we picked up speed again and stormed up Golborne bank, around Golborne Junction, and on towards Wigan, passing Bamfurling Junction at

69 miles per hour. Through Wigan station the speed dropped to 50 miles per hour for the station restriction and as we came up the 1 in 104 gradient of Boards Head bank we slowed still further to 41 miles per hour, nonetheless a pretty good rate of climb for this bank. Over the top at Coppull we went with the prospect of some more fast running. Euxton Junction was passed at 80 miles per hour, which rose to 85 as we flew through Farington. My thoughts went back to when I was a fireman on the shunts, dreamily watching the flyers go by, and wishing that I was up there on the footplate. Now the wheel had turned full circle in my career, the 'heaven' of my A4 footplate being someone else's dream.

There was plenty of time in hand as we ran through Preston, since we had covered the fifty-one miles from Crewe in fifty-one minutes, and we were now twelve minutes early. Later accounts of our run which appeared in the various railway magazines made the comment that the trip was spectacular, but criticised our speed. It was declared that we were asking for trouble with relation to other trains, possible collision, adverse effect upon the time-tables, etc. All this was nonsense, of course; obviously our critics knew nothing of British Rail's Weekly Notices of Special Train Arrangements, or else they ignored them. Every station and signal box along our route knew in advance of our journey, and both speed and delay allowances had been worked into our time-table. The signal men did all in their power to give us the right of way, but in any case I had to obey their signals—if that signal arm dropped I had only one course of action open to me—STOP.

We encountered signal checks from Preston to Barton and Broughton, but once the other train was safely inside the loop line at Garstang we were able to pick up speed again. The twelve minutes we had gained up to Preston were lost in these signal delays, whilst the twenty-one miles to Lancaster took us thirty-one minutes. Now we were slightly behind time. Carnforth was passed at 75 miles per hour but this dropped to 68 as we cleared the top of the bank.

My two firemen used their skills and knowledge of the road to the utmost, working perfectly as team between themselves as well as with me. The three of us enjoyed ourselves tremendously; to be honest, we were like three adult lads 'playing at trains' but with many years of experience behind us for sober guidance. The continual stream of passengers visiting us were finding the experience as 'something out of this world'. Without exception, all were exhilarated.

In comparison to our earlier speed we trundled through Oxenholme at a mere 48 miles per hour, and maintained that speed on the 1 in 131 gradient up to Grayrigg Bank. However the day being what it was, I had to ease the regulator a little to be sure of going round the reverse curves at Low Gill within the speed limit of 60 m.p.h. I could not afford to let regulations slip as both the Superintendent of the Line and the Shed Boss were passengers. We hurtled towards Dillicar Troughs at 75 miles per hour, and this time I

4498 tops Grayrigg Bank on the 1st April railtour. (Brian Stephenson)

was determined that there would be no mishaps, so everyone was cleared from the tender before the scoop was lowered for a successful fill of the tank.

'Sir Nigel Gresley' was running beautifully. With a maximum head of steam of 250lb p.s.i. and the boiler level showing full, we had perfect conditions for the assault on Shap Summit for which task the Train Arrangement notice, which I had read the night before, gave us an allowance of ten minutes. At this time a very kind gentleman brought us some tea from the restaurant car. That ambrosial liquid could not have been more welcome, nor tasted so good, had it been the nectar of the Gods. 4498 and ourselves were now ready for anything.

I opened the regulator to its limit and dropped the wheel a couple of turns, which resulted in a tremendous roar from the exhaust and wraiths of steam and smoke hanging to the echoes of the resonant chime which bounced along either side of the track. I was blowing the chime, not strictly regulation, for the benefit of the trackside tape recordists, several of which displayed banners carrying typical messages such as, "Please sound your whistle, driver. Tape recording in progress." Needless to say, I was only too pleased to comply with this request. About us, on either side, were literally hundreds of people waving and cheering; their joy and exuberance we could not hear, it being drowned in the thundering of our passage. I have never before, nor since, seen the bleak moorlands so densely populated, each member of the crowd being there with the common desire to pay homage to this fine locomotive. These spectators were of all ages and both sexes, and it was a marvel not only where came from, but in some cases, how they got there at all. Had I been alone, I am sure that I should have cried with sheer breath-taking happiness at this spontaneous gesture of the public; even so I had to swallow rather hard to clear the lump in my throat.

We passed the little signal box of Scout Green, our vibrations shaking the very foundation of the stone building. The signalman gave us a cheery grin and the 'thumbs up' sign. Of course, he had to have his joke; he slammed his fist into the palm of his other hand in rapid fashion, this being the universal sign on the railway that a banking engine is required. Cheeky fellow. But it was one of the multitude of things which were woven into the tapestry of this memorable occasion.

The sound of the engine was almost hypnotic, with the steady pounding and hissing of the pistons, the sturdy coughing of the exhaust, and the continuous song of the rails. We gave our own brand of sighs as we flew under the Bridge of Sighs and roared past Shap Summit, just one hundred and eleven miles out from home, and one hundred and twenty-seven minutes passed on the clock. We had climbed the bank in only six minutes fifty-eight seconds of our allotted ten minutes. Great. Now we had three minutes in hand, a bonus which we maintained all the way to Carlisle despite signal checks and permanent way restrictions.

Our arrival at Carlisle was heralded by my blowing of the chime, which was echoed back by every whistle and hooter in the yards, and brought throngs of people to the platform to mill around 'Sir Nigel Gresley'. In the midst of all the excitement Mr. Riddick came on aboard accompanying a lady. My two firemen and I were introduced to her, and for me this was one of the proudest moments of my entire career on the railway. The lady was Mrs. Godfrey, the daughter of the later Sir Nigel Gresley, the designer of the locomotive which bore his name, and of which I was now the driver. Rarely short for words, this was one occasion when I was tongue-tied, and happy to be so.

The train had been programmed to proceed to Kingmoor and continue in the down loop with the passengers still aboard so that they could take photographs. In the meantime we were to take the engine on to the shed for servicing; there she was to be turned ready for our return trip via Hellifield and Blackburn, and thence on to the main line at Farington Junction.

Soon it was time to depart, so with the passengers safely shepherded on board again we headed back into Carlisle on time; folks who had detrained in order to visit the city were picked up. As we left Carlisle behind, storm clouds oozed down from the hills, looking decidely black and ominous. I tried to race ahead of them but they were spreading all around. After passing Lazonby, the home of Sir Gerald Ley, in twenty-two minutes. I gave her a burst of speed, going really fast as we headed up through the Eden Valley to New Biggin. It was grand to feel all this power at my command, merely the turn of a wrist away.

Approaching Appleby, the distant signal was on, so I slammed the regulator shut and immediately applied the brakes to bring the speed down in readiness for stopping at the home signal. Just as were about to stop, the signal was lowered and the 'bobby' appeared on the signal box steps armed with a camera. All the other signals were in the clear position so it appeared that we had been delayed in order that this chap could take a photograph. This was against the regulations, but I couldn't really blame the man— probably I'd have wanted to do the same in his shoes. Nonetheless, in parting I gave him my blessing in the form of a time-honoured gesture familiar to all frustrated drivers!

By now the storm clouds had caught up with us and it was snowing quite heavily. I opened the regulator a little, but it was too much as the wheels slipped on the wet rails, racing furiously as they felt for a dry bite; instinctively, and in far less time than it takes to tell, I closed the regulator, opened the sanders, and re-opened the regulator. For about fifty yards she kept a grip on the track before slipping again. I repeated the actions, waiting until her frantic wheel thrashing has subsided, and then opened her out again, but she slipped once more on the snow covered rails. Our method of travel was almost like a ballroom dancing routine—slip . . . close . . . sand . . . grip . . . open . . . slip. In this fashion we continued up the heavy gradient from Ormside to Mallerstang. By now my arms felt as if they were made of cast iron and lead and my shoulders ached as though they were burning, all from the sheer physical exertion of continually opening and closing the regulator. But there was a more serious aspect to this adverse working. The boiler water level was getting lower and lower, and as Ais Gill Summit was reached I had to ease her right down to the minimum in order to recover our boiler level. The observers in the magazines described our descent from here as being leisurely, probably due to a shortage of steam, but I can affirm that at no time were we ever short of this. Because of the continual slipping we were using up water at an alarming rate, this in turn neccessitating me to take it easy across the levels of the moors.

On our arrival at Hellifield one or two passengers quickly left us, and soon we were on our way again, stopping at Blackburn for precious water. The water column here had been allowed to fall into a disgraceful state of disrepair, with the consequence that more water splashed onto the ground than went into our tank. This was most annoying, as the minutes ticked by and played havoc with our schedule, already some twenty minutes late. Accordingly, when the gauge registered three thousand five hundred gallons I decided that it would be enough to see us through to the Moore Troughs just south of Warrington, so to the good wishes and fond farewells of the spectators as Blackburn we set off again, heading for Pleasington and the run downhill to Farington Junction and the West Coast main line, and passing my old depot at Lostock Hall (how I would have loved to stand there and watch her go through). The 'Blue Lady' was back into her stride.

Despite the overcast skies she must have looked a splendid sight from the trackside, truly a symbol of dear old England, with her patriotic red, white, and blue train (red wheels, some old British Railways maroon coaches, white and blue British Rail Coach stock, and her own kingfisher blue livery.

We streaked past Leyland trailing plumes of steam, and roared through Euxton Junction around the 60 miles per hour mark, ready to set about tackling Coppull Bank. This she did in fine style, flinging herself over the top before beginning the descent to Wigan. The brakes were applied at 80 to take us through Wigan Station at 50 mph, then followed some fast running to Golborne Junction, which was taken at 60 to clear the points on the diverging tracks.

Going down the bank to Warrington Dick Howarth tapped an insistent finger on the water gauge. I nodded grimly, for I'd had my eye on it for some time—our water level in the tender was down to one thousand five hundred gallons. I grinned re-assuringly at him, saying that we should shortly make the next set of troughs. This we soon did, so as we approached the Moore Troughs, Dick dropped the water scoop, his eyes glued to the gauge. At the start the water level registered one thousand gallons but by the time we cleared there was even less showing. We didn't pick up a bucketful, so it was a case of 'Crewe or bust'!

The level was down to eight hundred gallons as we passed through Weaver Junction, with Dick agitatedly reminding me of this fact. "Don't keep looking at the gauge, Dick. The more you look the worse it will get. It'll only keep dropping." So saying, I promptly covered the gauge with a cloth.

As I remember it, we arrived at Crewe a good (or should I say bad?) forty minutes late, and my two firemen and myself were relieved in more ways than one. Later on I talked to the relief driver. "Bert," he said "you had a narrow squeak with 'Sir Nigel Gresley', didn't you?" I didn't quite 'cotton-on' to what he meant. "How do you mean?", I asked.

"Well, when I relieved you on Saturday night we took her onto the South shed, and just as we arrived on the water column road the injectors knocked off. The water tank was bone dry."

I put on a mock superior manner, and with tongue in cheek I replied, "Yes, it was pretty good judgement, wasn't it?"

My next encounter with the 'Blue Lady' was just over two months later when, on 9th June, 1967, I was detailed to bring 4498 from Nine Elms depot back up to Crewe South shed, after a successful tour on the Southern Region. We travelled as passengers to Willesden and went along to Acton Lane signal box to await her arrival. Time passed and still no sign of her. Doubts began to fill my mind—Had I come on the right day? Had there been an accident? I decided to contact movements control who told me that her original booked time of arrival had been altered and that other arrangements had been made. Apparently it was not considered safe for her to travel under the electrified wires, and so she had been re-routed; these new arrangements had been made before we left Crewe, but no-one had thought to tell us. This was just another example of the frequent lapses of liaison between Control and the Motive Power Depots. Everyone except the staff directly involved seemed to be aware of what was supposed to be happening at any given time. I felt that, if only just this once, some-one had to be trimmed down to size, so the startled controller at the other end of the phone felt the verbal force of my wrath, and wriggled away saying that he would make further enquiries. I then waited so long that I thought he had gone off for his holidays, but eventually he returned, asking me first if I was still there, and then informing me that 4498 was being sent direct up to Acton Lane. "Are you sure that she will be O.K. under the wires?" he asked. Keeping my cool (after all, he was not to know of my personal experience with the locomotive) I told him that she had been driven under the wires without mishap. He seemed satisfied with this assurance and told me that 4498 would be with me in half an hour. One hour and forty-five minutes later she arrived.

My pleasure was more than a little dimmed when I saw her, for I was horrified at the terribly depressing state she was in, with a thin film of oil and muck covering everything from cabside to gauge glasses; I don't think that she had been wiped or cleaned since she had left Crewe, it certainly looked that way. Therefore, during a twenty minute wait for the road onto the main line at Willesden Junction, my mate on this occasion, Albert Hassall, and myself managed to spruce her up a bit.

The locomotive had been brought to us supposedly in full running order, but the bunker and the water tank were half empty whilst the crumbled coal that was in the tender was the remnants of her last run on the Southern Region; it was like powder, and as we gathered speed the dust swirled around us. My mate continually swilled down in a desperate effort to keep things clean and tidy, but our distress was further aggravated by the fact that at this time there were no water troughs left in existence between London and Crewe. All that remained to record the once glorious days of steam were a few isolated water columns.

On our arrival at Bletchley the signalman at the power box asked if we were alright for water. I told him that we had filled up at Willesden and could manage until we got to Rugby, but he suggested that we could fill up at Bletchley. A few rapid calculations convinced me that if we took advantage of his offer we should carry enough to take us to Crewe, anyway there was always the water supply at Lichfield or Stafford in case of emergency. So we trundled off into the carriage sidings for water. Then an incident occurred, small in itself, but the memory of which still rankles and leaves a nasty taste in my mouth. Almost before you could say, "4498", we were surrounded by a host of spectators. They were railwaymen of all grades, all departments, but predominantly loco men, as one might expect with a foreign engine making an appearance on their road. It was obvious from the manner of their approach and comments that they were not steam men, for by now some of·them would not have had the chance to ride on steam. But in this new breed of railway man there was always one who thought it 'big' to make derogatory remarks about steam engines; this group at Bletchley was no exception. One chap called up to us, "Where are you taking her?" To which I replied that we were heading for Crewe. "What for, are they going to break her up? Should have done it years ago instead of leaving them lying around cluttering up the place, coal dust everywhere." I could have punched him in the face for his churlish remarks, but contented myself with sending him packing with a few choice English words ringing in his ears. He was obviously a man softened up by the coming of the diesels and the electrics!

At any rate, thanks to the kind concern of the power box man at Bletchley, on that June evening in 1967, we arrived at Crewe South shed at 6.00 p.m. with an ample supply of water still left in the tank.

The 'Blue Lady', with Bert leaning out of the cab, passes through Lichfield Trent Valley station after the Bletchley water stop.

I had to wait until the end of October in that same year before I had the pleasure once again of standing on the footplate of the 'Blue Lady'. On this occasion, the 28th, the Railway Correspondence and Travel Society organised a run from Nottingham to Carlisle, the name of the train for the day being 'The Border Limited'. Once more I had Neil Cadman as my mate, with Leslie Jackson as second fireman. The tour arrived at Crewe diesel hauled and was greeted by a few half-hearted claps from the crowds waiting on the platform—more jeers than cheers, I reckon. What a different story when 4498 backed onto the train. The enthusiasts, who to judge by their numbers must have just about exhausted British Rail's stock of platform tickets, greeted her with a continuous wall of sound, built of ear-splitting cheers and thunderous hand-clapping. Above this din I thought I could hear the sound of the commercial men of British Rail rubbing their hands together as the piles of pennies in the coffers was counted.

We left Crewe in grand style, and in just ten minutes from a dead start we were speeding along at a thunderous 96 miles per hour, pushing hard for the 'ton'. However, as we approached Weaver Junction we had a double yellow signal against us; I cursed at our bad luck of not reaching the magic 100 miles per hour. Perhaps it was as well, for soon after I had to reduce speed as we cleared electrified section and ran onto the 90 miles per hour limit tracks. The twenty-four miles from Crewe to Warrington were accomplished in twenty-two minutes forty seconds—not bad going at all. From Warrington to Preston we had a variety of signal checks and delays, the journey taking longer than had been anticipated; for the twenty-seven miles we had to be satisfied with an average speed of 40½ miles per hour. It seemed so slow compared to the earlier part of our run that I remember thinking that we could have probably walked it as quick.

It is probably true to say that speed is an insistent drug, and certainly I have always revelled in it. Some of the greatest thrills in my life have been on the footplate of a speeding locomotive with me pushing her pushing me pushing her, etc. Always I have been a stickler for safety rules and regulations, but equally so I always kept an eye open for the main chance, as it were. Probably the Jekyll and Hyde in me, I suppose. Certainly, as we pulled away from Preston after picking up passengers, my head was full of thoughts.

For this particular section the timings were a little generous, one hundred and eighteen minutes being allowed for the trip. However, I decided that we would knock spots off these times and give the rail fans something to remember for a long time. We roared through Garstang at a gratifying 84 miles per hour and feeling very pleased, only to have the smile rubbed off my face with two permanent way checks, one at Scorton and the second at Lancaster No. 1. These two cost cost us eight and a half minutes.

Lancaster Station was able to take a leisurely view of us as we came down the bank, through the station, and on over the River Lune bridge. I was not pushing 4498 at this stage, just keeping her average speed around the 60 mark. The heaviest part of our journey lay ahead and I wanted my firemen to have every advantage possible in readiness for the onslaught. In this fashion we continued onto and through Carnforth. Then I opened her up and we fairly flew up the incline towards Burton and Holme. Our speed at this point was 74 miles per hour, which I raised to 79 by the time we reached Milnthorpe. The start of Grayrigg Bank had begun in fine style. The official distance between Milnthorpe and Grayrigg Bank is registered at 12.6 miles, and we accomplished that stretch in just twelve minutes seven seconds. I have often wondered whether this constitutes something of a record for three cylinder locomotives. Perhaps one day some railway statistician-cum-historian will delve into the science which deals with such subjects and come up with an answer. I know that faster times have been recorded, notably with 6244 King George VI hauling the 10.05 out from London Euston during the war, but she was a larger engine.

Now came the assault on Shap. As we roared through Tebay at 70 miles per hour Neil and Leslie gave me the 'thumbs up' sign. "O.K., Bert. Get at it", they choroused. I answered with a grin, and then gave her head. She responded magnificently. The noise from the exhaust was terrific as we started the 1 in 75 climb between mileposts 31½ and 37½, our speed being in the middle fifties. Someone told us afterwards that a figure of 2,550 had been calculated for the equivalent draw-bar horse-power for this four miles ascent. It was certainly the fastest that I have done over Shap, even with a diesel. Going down the bank from the Summit I held her back a little. I could afford this little breather, so to speak, since our allowance from Preston to Shap Summit was eighty minutes, and we had accomplished it in only sixty-five minutes. With such an amount of time in hand I wanted to give the lads a bit of a break, as well as the engine, and also to give them chance to prepare for a good burst of speed on the last lap of the journey.

Once we had passed Penrith we started to move fast, like a blue bullet. Plumpton whizzed by at 84 miles per hour, then we raced along the short open stretch and up the slight embankment to Calthwaite, the snaking River Petteril below and seemingly trying to beat us to the now dis-used station. Our speed reached 88 miles per hour and we streaked through the station clear winners, the river curling away in acknowledgement of our superiority. We soon arrived at Carlisle, passing the no. 13 home signal, eighty-eight miles from Preston, in a time of eighty-seven minutes forty-three seconds. In other words, we finished up seventeen seconds over the half the hour ahead of our schedule. I don't reckon that there'll be many passengers who will claim that they didn't get value for money that day!

There had been a strong rumour circulating around Crewe just before we had left with the special that this would be the last time that 4498 would be run over any British Rail main line. Of course, we dismissed the rumour as ludicrous, but like most rumours, there is always the germ of the truth some where. In the event it was not the last time that 'Sir Nigel Gresley' ran on British Rail's tracks, but certainly thereafter she languished for months on end in Crewe South shed.

Chapter XII
A BRUSH WITH THE ARTIST

We hold these truths to be sacred and undeniable; that all men are created equal and independent, that from that equal creation they derive rights inherent and inalienable, among which are the preservation of life, and liberty, and the pursuit of happiness.

Original draft for the
Declaration of Independence, 4th July 1776

Roman, be this thy care—these thine arts—to bear dominion over the nations and to impose the law of peace, to spare the humbled and to wear down the proud.

Aeneid, vi, 851.
Virgil 70—19 B.C.

Those two quotations, centuries apart, might have been originally made with David Shepherd, the famous wildlife painter and steam locomotive preservationist, in mind. The guiding light of David, through his art, is the preservation, in mind. The guiding light of David, through his art, is the preservation of (wild)life, the pursuit of happiness, and the sparing of the humbled (scrap-yard steam locomotives).

Principally known for his paintings of wild life, David Shepherd has a second love, that of steam locomotives. He has preserved several of his own in full working order, and has immortalised many more on his canvases. The almost photographic realism of his paintings contain that extra undefineable ingredient—total rapport with the subject. One of his most famous paintings shows a scene of dereliction and decay at Nine Elms motive power depot at the end of the steam era. Surrounded by piles of rubble, ash spilling over from in-filled inspection pits, tangled cables and discarded firing irons and signal lamps, a BR Class 5 4-6-0 stands in rust-coated dejection. Even though she lacks much of her motion, someone has indelicately chalked on a cylinder casing 'For Sale—9/6d and 3000 Green Stamps', but this once proud locomotive still retains her dignity, ignoring the cruelty of her reflection in a pool of rusty water, and the impertinence of the flowering weeds which stand watching her.

My first encounter with David came in the line of duty. Reporting in on 4th April, 1968, I was informed that my shed boss, Mr. Dentith, wanted to see me. Curiousity aroused, I knocked at his office door, and a voice called for me to enter. On doing so, I knew that all was well, because I didn't have to stand on the carpet, instead I was invited to sit down.

"Bert, have you ever heard of David Shepherd?"

"Oh yes, he's a parson fellow who plays cricket for England."

"No, this chap's an artist", Mr. Dentith replied.

"In that case, I've never heard of him", I said.

Mr. Dentith proceeded to rectify the omissions in my artistic education. "Well, the position is this. Mr. Shepherd has purchased two locomotives—a Class 9F, No. 92203, and a Class 4MT tender engine. On the 6th April they are to be moved from Crewe to Longmoor Military Camp, and I would like you to take them as far as Derby. Mr. Shepherd will be riding with you, along with a Mr. Barnes from Granada T.V." My eyebrows reached skyward and my mouth dropped open. What could I say!

So on the 6th April I duly booked on for duty at 5.30 hours on a rather cold morning. 92203 would need some lengthy preparation for the road to Derby, and I was glad that Neil Cadman had been assigned for firing duty on her. We had hardly set about our respective tasks when we were joined by a young chap dressed in blue overalls and sporting a regulation black peaked cap. He kept up an incessant chatter about the engine, and steam locomotives in general, as I worked my way round the 2-10-0. He also seemed to know his way round the engine, and was as eager as a beaver. Every now and then, just as I thought I was going to be able to get a word in edgeways, the fellow would punctuate his words with a most musical laugh. After a while an opportunity presented itself and I escaped, making my way to Neil who was tending the fire. I gave him a nudge, making sure that we were alone, and said, "Who the heck is this bloke, Neil?" My mate could only shake his head. As I then looked down from the cab, I could see this mysterious person inspect something between the wheels. He turned and grinned, and then resumed his inspection. I couldn't figure him out at all; his dress and chatter suggested that he was a new fireman on his first day—but surely that couldn't be. I was perplexed.

At that moment, Mr. Dentith made an appearance, having come across from his office. He knew the fellow, and all smiles, went straight to him, shook his hand, and stood talking to him for a while. Then he introduced our talkative companion as the owner of the engine; no wonder he knew his way around her!

On this day, as on the others when I had the pleasure of being in his company, I found him to be a veritable dynamo, always on the go; he could wear out any ordinary mortal who merely stood watching him. The sheer exuberance of his enthusiasm was contagious, and on that cold April morning his tremendous excitement at the prospect of having his own steam locomotives working conveyed itself to us all. He was most anxious to be off so as to arrive at Longmoor as soon as possible.

We departed from Crewe South Shed at 7.00 am, having been joined on the footplate by our Divisional Superintendent, Mr. McMurdie, suitably attired in overalls and peaked cap. From the array of uniforms it certainly looked as if we shouldn't go short of someone to drive the engine. Once clear of the depot, I decided to pull this artist fellow's leg a little; he looked like the sort of chap who could take a joke. I tipped the wink at Mr. McMurdie, and turned to David.

"I presume you have permission from the A4 Locomotive Society for us to man your engines today, David?"

He frowned in puzzlement, looked hard at me, and tried to fathom out what I was talking about. But I kept a straight face as I continued, "You see, the A4 people have us under contract, and hire us out to British Rail on occasions like this. I suppose that they will be charging you a substantial fee for our services." Neil could no longer contain himself and burst out laughing. David realised that he been spoofed, and promptly picked up the firing shovel, threatening to brain me with it.

By this time we were well away from the depot, so I considered it safe to placate David by giving him his head, so to speak. I slid out of the driving seat, saying to him, "Come on, it's your engine, you may as well drive her." Enthusiasm is one thing, but knowing one's limitations is another, and David declined the offer, although I am sure that he would dearly have liked to handle the regulator. He explained that he had not had much experience over this particular road, which is reason enough, even for a seasoned driver. So I extended the invitation to our Divisional Superintendent. He needed no second asking, and the speed with which he accepted gave me the impression that he had been impatiently waiting for the chance since Crewe. He took over the controls, and I left him in charge; in point of fact, this was how we arrived at Derby, with the gaffer still driving.

We stopped at Derby (London Road Junction) where the relief crew were to take over. They were there ready for us, along with a footplate inspector, so as soon as they were safely on board, Mr. McMurdie opened the regulator, his intention being to take us into the station proper. But there was no response from 92203—the valve gear was pulled too far back. He closed the regulator and tried again; still no movement from the engine. I discreetly made signs to him to shut the regulator and drop the wheels a little. Not a word was spoken, but the Super. took the hint, and with the regulator closed he dropped the wheel. This had the desired effect of movement, but because the steam had built up in the cylinders with such pressure, she slipped wildly. This caused the footplate inspector to turn to me with an angry frown on his face and say, "What sort of a driver is this? I did not speak, but just pointed at the Divisional Superintendent, who of course, had been aware of the exchange. With all the solemnity of his rank the inspector turned to Mr. McMurdie and asked, "Are you the driver of this engine?" to which the reply was an emphatic "No". Now the inspector began to show his mettle. Here was a flagrant case of some unauthorised person driving a locomotive on British Rail's metals—this was against regulations, and he had caught the culprit in the act. Strictly to the letter of the law, he was right. Sternly, he once more rounded on me, and coldly enquired, "Who is supposed to be the driver of this engine?"

Like a young lad caught with his hand in the apple barrel, I meekly answered, "I am." He flung out his arm, his finger pointing stiffly across the cab, "Well, just who the hell is that driving?"

I shook my head, looking innocent, "Do you know, I haven't the faintest idea. You'd better ask him."

By now the inspector had really got the bit between his teeth, and rarin' to tear a strip off us all. Within the confines of the cab he gave a good impression of an angry R.S.M. marching across the parade ground. He turned to the Divisional Superintendent, and barked, "What's your name, and where are you from?"

Casually, without a sound, and without a twitch of his face, Mr. McMurdie produced an identity card from his pocket and handed it to the irate inspector. The look on his face beggared description, and I thought he would burst a blood vessel. To his credit, he completed his statutory task, scrutinising the document thoroughly before handing it back. He realised he had been 'had', and there were profuse apologies all round.

Mr. McMurdie did get the locomotive moving properly and we reached Derby Station in good order where, after numerous photographs had been taken, we bade farewell to the two engines and the man who had saved them from the cutters torch.

In September of that year, Neil and I were invited to David Shepherd's beautiful home in Surrey, and during the weekend we were able to see the film of ourselves and the two engines on the journey from Crewe. In contrast to David, who is always on the go, his charming wife was so cool, calm, and collected. There were about twenty or so men roaming all over the place and messing about with engines, but she didn't turn a hair.

It was while I was here that I met Dr. Peter Beet, of Steamtown, Carnforth fame. During the Saturday evening, David put on a cine show, which included a film featuring the scrapyard at Barry, and showed the once proud locomotives being carved up by the breakers' acetylene torches. The Doctor made a comment, which to the lover of steam engines, really says it all—"I'd rather perform a post-mortem than watch this."

This statement typifies the love that David, and all other preservationists have for steam locomotives. Perhaps more than others, David is able to demonstrate his passion for preservation, since he is also an active member of the Wild Life Trust. At every opportunity he seizes the chance to use his art for the benefit of lovers of wild life and railways everywhere.

In his foreword to this book, David calmly mentions a run of an Inter-City Electric from Crewe to Euston, and return. Now it can be told, he says. By golly, now it can be told, indeed. Up to that fateful day I hadn't a grey hair in my head, and now all my friends call me 'Snowy'.

On the 1st November, 1969, David and a friend received official permission to ride with me on an electric locomotive from Crewe to London and return. Out from Crewe at 3.54 p.m. this train also carried on board the anonymous inspector referred to in the foreword; his name is H★rry M★rg★n. Our first stop was Rugby, then Watford, then Euston. When we were clear of Rugby I invited our guests to take turns driving the train. David's friend, Mr. Selway, had the first chance, and with me standing beside him giving instructions, he became quite well acquainted with the driving technique. David then took his turn and was doing alright too, when at 100 miles per hour, two yellow signals loomed up. I rapped out the command to David, "Run her down." This didn't mean that there was a cow on the line and I wanted him to drive at her; it meant that he had to run power off the traction motors, then close the controller, and apply the brakes. He understood me correctly, and closed the controller alright, but in his haste to obey me, and because of his unfamiliarity with the control panel layout, he forgot the position of the brake handle. For what seemed like an eternity his hands waved all over the place, but I quickly reached across him and applied the brakes. Our speed was reduced as per regulations, but the next signal was green so in no time at all we were doing 100 once more.

I will say this from him—as an engine driver he makes a jolly good artist!

Cricklewood shed plays host to 92203 and 75029 during their journey to Longmoor.
(Peter Nicholson)

Wild life preserved at Derby Midland station! From left to right: Mr. Dentith, Robert McMurdie, David Shepherd, Bert Stewart, Bill Hughes, Neil Cadman, and an un-identified fireman.

Chapter XIII
TALES OF THE TRACKS

By the end of August 1967, I was back at work ater that most enjoyable holiday in Canada. My first job was to take a diesel up to Carlisle, from where a relief crew would work it back south to Liverpool Exchange on the 9.00 a.m. from Glasgow, whilst I was to return to Crewe working the 'Royal Scot' bound for London. Whenever I worked this train, either going north from Crewe, or going south from Carlisle, there was one stage of the road that was guaranteed to send nostalgic memories flooding through my mind. That place was Farrington and my mind would go back in time to those seeming far-off days when I was a young fireman. My hopes and dreams would all be re-lived and I would say to myself, "Well, lad, you've made it."

I am always conscious of the rich heritage of experiences to be found on the railway—if only the tracks could tell tales, what a wonderfully rich human saga they would record. Ever mindful of my own humble beginnings, and a natural aversion to pomposity, I could never resist the urge to take down a peg or two those individuals who stood on their dignity a little too much.

I remember travelling on a Preston to Crewe train just before my wife and I moved to Crewe. A ticket inspector moved along the early morning train, his insistent call, "All tickets, please" echoing through the compartments and breaking into the peaceful slumber of some of the passengers. Without comment he examined the proffered tickets and handed them back until, that is, he came to me. Dressed in full footplate uniform I was a stranger on his run, and in contrast to his almost disinterested attention to the other passengers, he rather curtly enquired of me, "Where are you going?"

Being used to a cheery nod and a few exchanges of pleasant conversation from fellow railwayman, I was a little startled, so replied, "What do you want to know for? You didn't ask these other passengers about their destination."

Now very haughty, he said, "No, but they did show me their tickets." I agreed that it was his job to ask, and suggested that it might have been more courteous to ask to see mine. My gentle protests at his attitude evidently suggested to him that he had caught me travelling without my pass, but then his cold authoritarian manner changed abruptly to red-faced embarassment when I calmly produced the necessary pass, all much to the amusement of my fellow passengers. It was with the greatest difficulty that I managed to keep a straight face as he hurriedly strode from the compartment. However I must say that I found his pompous sort a minority among the many hundreds of inspectors that I met during my career.

Everyone has a job to do, but there are way to do it, and way not to, when dealing with other people. Perhaps the ticket collector could have learned a lesson from the locomotive inspector I met on my first job to Glasgow in November, 1965. Because of the fog from Carlisle I drove the Brush Sulzer Type 4 into Glasgow three minutes late. It was a regular procedure for arrivals there from the south to be met by a locomotive inspector who enquired for details of delays and locomotive defects. The inspector who met my train pleasantly asked the reason for the delay, so I simply told him of the fog from Carlisle to Beattock Summit. "O.K., Bert, I'll make the necessary checks. Cheerio." I know which fellow railwayman I would have the time for again.

On that same run, my second man and myself booked off duty at Polmadie shed and then made our way to the enginemens hostel at Gushett Falls. This was one of many primitive buildings British Rail optimistically called 'hostels'. Men, tired from a heavy day's run, were expected to sleep easily amid all manner of noises which one would expect from a closely inhabited tenement district. Coalmen, about to deliver their bulky black cargo, would blow a horn to announce their arrival; it was like being at a staging post in the old coaching days, and as if that were not enough, the milkmen blew whistles (calling up the cows for a refill?)! Then there were the men from Carlisle Kingmoor depot; these men had the most raucous voices that I think I ever heard. We at Crewe always used to reckon that if you heard a Kingmoor man speaking with a quiet voice it was a dead certainty that he'd had an operation on his throat.

Railwaymen, especially footplate staff, are always ready for a joke. So, one day in November, 1965, just after my first job to Glasgow, the 8.45 a.m. from Carlisle arrived at Crewe and was formed of steam heat only stock. For southbound passenger trains at this time it was the practice to double head this type of carriage with a boilered locomotive sandwiched between the main train engine and the coaches. This arrangement was in operation to Nuneaton, the southern limit of electric traction at the time.

For this job I had a handsome 'Black Five' whilst a more senior colleague looked after the electric locomotive that was to lead. After the formality of coupling up, the old driver came along to my footplate, and with a grin, said, "I'll try not to go too fast for you, driver." Nonchalantly I replied, "Just please yourself how fast you go." This comment took a little wind from his sails.

We started away and before long were speeding along in the 80's. I had just a breath of steam on, for that was all that was required, and as I looked along the side of the loco the motion was just a thrashing blur. With our run being non-stop to Nuneaton, barring signal checks, this meant that we would trundle along as fast as we liked, which in fact was what happened.

As we ran into Nuneaton Station I took a pack of playing cards from out of my haversack, and said to my mate, "Make haste, Bob. Come over here and we'll have a little fun." I arranged a shovel over our haversacks, put a handful of loose change at the side, dealt a couple of hands, then, after taking a quick look out of the cab, sat down with my mate. In due course the electric driver hastened along to our footplate, grinning all over his face. His merriment was short-lived, however.

"Queen takes Jack, and I've got the master trump", I said as he climbed aboard. To say the very least, he looked non-plussed; to him here was a game of cards well in progress, with all the stakes laid out at the side. I looked up in feigned surprise. "Crikey, are we at Nuneaton already? Just my luck. I was on a winning streak too."

The driver was dumbstruck, lost for words, and without uttering a single one he turned round, climbed down, and walked back to his engine shaking his head. "That shook him, Bert", said my mate, trying in vain to keep his laughter under control!

I remember going down to London once, with my mate, working a late running service from Carlisle, which we picked up at Crewe. We arrived at Euston Station at about 3 o'clock, just in time to catch the 3.05 p.m. to Liverpool. I snatched a quick wash in the toilet and then, with my tea can at the ready, made my way down the train to the kitchen-car for a brew. As I passed through the restaurant car on the way, a dear old lady looked up from her meal, eyed me over the top of her spectacles, and enquired, "Are you the driver, young man?"

With my tongue in my cheek I answered, "Yes, ma'am." She looked puzzled for a moment, then asked, "Well, if that is so, who is driving now you are here?"

With a dead-pan face that would have done credit to a professional poker player I replied, "You see, ma'am, this locomotive has done the journey so often that it knows where it is going, without me to tell it."

"How spendid. My how British Rail have progressed in this last decade."

With that little bit of gay repartee over with I continued with my journey in quest of that for which everything is alleged to stop—tea. But I still wonder who was having who in that pleasant exchange.

As you may have guessed already from this book, engine drivers are funny folks. I always used to derive quite a lot of amusement from the simple pastime of observing my fellow workmates. One of the drivers at Lostock Hall used to chain smoke from the start of a journey right through to the end, but the odd thing was that he never smoked anywhere else, even at home. One day I happened to ride with him to Todmorden on an early morning train which we had relieved at Preston. The moment he climbed aboard he lit up with the first, smoked it to the nub end, and instead of throwing this among the coal or into the fire, he dropped it onto the footplate. Then he started on the next cigarette, and the next . . . until the footplate was littered. This annoyed me intensely because I always prided myself on keeping a clean footplate. I said nothing, but just swept them all up and put them into the bucket, intending at the end of the day to give him a shock by showing him how much litter he had thrown around. I asked him how many fags he thought he had smoked. "Oh, about fifty," was his casual reply. The bucket was emptied and I counted seventy. Was he surprised, astounded, shocked? Not in the least. He simply made the comment that he would see if he could manage to smoke eighty on the morrow. Oh well!

Every driver has his favourite stance or method of easing the strain and tensions which one encounters on the footplate. One chap I knew never used to sit down, no matter what engine he was driving. Instead he would stand, elbows resting on the cabside window ledge, with his head thrust through the aperture, resulting at the end of the day with his face as black as the ace of spades! Another Crewe driver continually bounced up and down on his seat no matter how smoothed the ride—he probably thought he was the Galloping Major!

One of my own methods for relaxing is singing—at least, that's what I call it. But in the days that followed my trip to Nine Elms depot to bring 4498 back to Crewe there was little to sing about. Things were pretty much of a day to day routine, running fast trains to London or Carlisle, or just plodding on with coal trains to Stoke and back. But the picture became very much brighter on the 15th October, 1967.

I was detailed for duty as driver on an enthusiasts' special chartered by the Stephenson Locomotive Society. We had BR standard 4-6-2 'Britannia' class locomotive 70013 'Oliver Cromwell' as our engine, which had the doubtful honour of being the last steam locomotive to be repaired at Crewe works, being despatched in February, 1967. This event is not to be confused with the last steam locomotive to be constructed at Crewe, class 9F 2-10-0 no. 92250, which left the works on 15th December, 1958, driven by the Mayor of Crewe, Councillor Tom Consterdine, a former railwayman.

On this trip with 'Oliver Cromwell' my mate was once again Neil Cadman; together we have done a few thousand miles and we have a perfect understanding between us. I rate him as one of the cleanest firemen I have ever worked with, for he never leaves any loose pieces of coal littering the footplate, and after every stint with the shovel the floor is meticulously swept clean and thoroughly swilled off with water. In my book he is the perfect fireman—his knowledge is geared to the ability to use it, both being blended to a very likeable personalilty.

The special train was extremely light, being composed of eight coaches of some two hundred and sixty four tons in weight, whilst our route lay through Blackburn and Hellifield, with the first stop Carlisle.

Everything was going to plan as we left Hellifield and began roaring up the 'Long Drag'. Neil came across to me and reported that the injectors were putting more water on the ballast than in the boiler. There seemed to be no immediate cause for concern, but as we made further progress up the incline it became increasingly apparent that we should soon have to stop, and this we did at Blea Moor. While Neil went to the signal box to explain our predicament to the 'bobby' and thereby protect our rear, I quickly dismantled the injectors. The sieves were absolutely full of ash and dirt—how we had managed to travel so far I will never know. I cleaned them out, re-assembled the injector, tested it, and things worked perfectly once more with no further trouble. The big disappointment of the whole trip was that high-speed running was out the question due to Sunday permanent way operations being in progress over the entire route.

My career on the footplate has shown me that disappointments can eventually provide a source of satisfaction. Two episodes, both of which were shared with Neil Cadman and 4498, illustrate this point.

The first was the memorable run on 28th October, 1967, when 4498 hauled the 'Border Limited' for the R.C.T.S. between Crewe and Carlisle. Because of policy statements by British Rail it was expected that this would be the last run by 4498 on British Rail metals. However a letter to me, dated three days later, shows how that run (described in Chapter XI), which started under a cloud, managed to give pleasure. The letter, from Philip Heald, reads:

Dear Bert,

I wish to thank you, most sincerely, for your kindness in allowing Julian (Riddick) and I have to have the most memorable day we have ever had in our lives. A day that I shall never ever forget. By all accounts the northbound run created new records which I do not suppose will ever be matched by a steam locomotive. I hope that it was just as thrilling for you, Neil and Les (Jackson).

If, by virtue of the Board's recent statements, the run was the last, it must surely be classed as a fitting finale, although I am just a little optimistic that one day common sense will win, and we shall be able to light up again.

Till we meet again—my sincere thanks for everything.

Yours sincerely
Philip

This is a letter which will always be treasured amongst my souvenirs.

The second run, which dispelled momentarily the gloomy forecasts of October, was on the 31st July, 1968, when Neil Cadman and I took 'Sir Nigel Gresley', running light engine, as far as Carlisle on her way to Philadelphia Colliery in County Durham. We were accompanied by Julian Riddick and Philip Heald on what we knew, at that time, to be the last run on British Rail. However, even with this fear-filled trip, both Julian and Philip, together with all the other officers and members of the A4 Locomotive Society Limited, maintained as unshakeable confidence in their hopes that one day 4498 would again grace our railways with her presence. Their faith was later justified.

I still have a copy of the British Railways (London Midland Region) Special Notice no. 866 G, relating to this journey which brings the memories flooding back. The time-table for the run is itemised and followed by the note "Crewe South Shed men to Carnforth, HP/AR." Because of an incident which I will recall in a moment, Neil and I fulfilled the duties as laid down in the second note which reads, "Carnforth men relieve 0N00 at 10.00 work to Kingmoor, HP/AR." So, as per time-table we departed Crewe at 7.00 a.m. and arrived at Bamfurlong Junction at 08.05 a.m. for a scheduled stop of twenty minutes, which among other things, allowed plenty of photographs to be taken and served to remind us of a prior arrangement made with a film crew. We kept our side of the bargain and it was funny to watch them keeping theirs. At a point on the M6 motorway just north of Preston, which runs parallel with the railway, the film crew had feigned a breakdown on the hard shoulder whilst awaiting our arrival. As we approached this rendezvous at about 65 mph we gave a pre-arranged signal with our chime whistle. From a distance it was funny to see them scrambling around, slamming the bonnet down, piling into the car and getting themselves and their equipment lined up and organised, whilst the driver concentrated on getting up to a matching speed as we quickly drew level with them. I later saw the film they had made and I regard it as a worthy record of their endeavours and their drill. It does them credit.

Our arrival at Carnforth M.P.D. was marred a little by the attitude of the relief driver and fireman. As soon as we stopped, the driver looked up at us from the ballast and said in a heavily contemptuous tone of voice, "Where is this load of junk going? I thought I had finished with these things."

If looks could kill he would have dropped dead on the spot as I fixed him with an icy glare, and retorted. "Mister, as far as I am concerned, you have finished with these engines. You don't need to come aboard. I can do what has to be done till the men taking her to County Durham show up. So, be on your way."

With a complete turn-round in attitude and a much more friendly tone to his voice, he said, "Now driver, don't get upset. How was I to know your feelings towards this loco'?"

I scarcely need add that Neil and myself stayed with 4498 through to Carlisle Kingmoor where a more amiable set of men took over, accompanied by a real gentlemen of a footplate inspector. They surely would look after my 'Blue Lady'.

Chapter XIV
THOUGHTS AT THE END OF THE LINE

It was not until I came to write these memoirs and set my thoughts on paper that I began to appreciate the magnitude of the task I had set myself. Thoughts crowded in thick and fast with one leading to another, perhaps not in chronological order or with any apparent connection between them. From the comfort of my home, and its relative peace and quiet, above the 'Sebastopol Inn', Chorley, I am tempted to observe that my career can be summed up in the phrase "From 5X to XXX", if you'll pardon the witticism.

By the end of 1969 the evolution, nay revolution, of the railways was complete. The electrics and diesels had taken over from the steam locomotives, their drivers and secondmen going to work 'dressed to kill'. Such was the sophistication of the new railwayman that polished plastic 'leather' shoes replace the hob-nailed boots and smartly tailored suits became the regulation uniform instead of the greasy overalls. Where once the footplateman had been recognised by a gaudy neckerchief tucked down the collar of his winceynette shirt, he was now to be seen wearing a fashionable nylon shirt and tie. A far cry indeed from the smoke, steam, coal dust and associated scruffiness of former days, of which I loved practically every glorious, hard-working, hard-playing minute. I would not have changed them for the world.

On occasions, I travelled up to County Durham and drove my beloved 'Blue Lady' (by kind permission of the A4 Society, of course) and recalled many memories of these wonderful days. As I sat on the driver's stool I thought of my steam days on British Rail, and of those famous drivers who had sat there before me coaxing the peak performance from this blue giant. I smiled to myself as I thought how I, and countless hundreds of drivers before me had coaxed and cursed, sweated and sworn at an engine in an attempt to locate the source of some malfunction. No reliance on electronic wizardry for us.

At about the time I first met David Shepherd, just prior to the last days of steam, there were in the London Midland Region a spate of troubles involving hot axle boxes on freight trains. In my humble opinion, a contributory cause was undoubtedy the sustained speeds of 45 miles per hour which were achieved quite easily by the diesel and electric locomotives, where as a steam engine hauling a similar train would probably drop down to 25 miles per hour when negotiating an incline, the slower speed thereby allowing any heated axle boxes to cool. Coupled with a lack of, perhaps reduced, maintenance, trouble was bound to occur. I am sure that the Carriage and Wagon Department would hotly contest this latter point, explaining as they did then, that some drivers ran in excess of the 45 miles per hour limit.

But whatever the cause, British Rail installed several hot-box detectors throughout the Region. A train running over this equipment with hot-box trouble would electronically trigger off a signal which indicated the location of the faulty vehicle in the train, and also whether the offending hot box was on the near-side or the off-side.

But of course, like all such apparatus, it has its fallible moments. For instance. One day I was working a through freight train to Willesden, and on approaching Rugby, where this equipment is installed, the signals were at the green aspect and I was set for a good run. However when the last wagon had cleared the detectors the next signal suddenly changed from green to two yellow. As we approached these, the two yellows changed to one, and finally I received the red signal at which I stopped. Immediately I got on the phone to enquire why the signals had been reversed against me. I was staggered when the signalman said, "Driver, you have forty-eight waggons on your train and each one has a hot axle box. I'll put you inside at Rugby for examination."

Inwardly cursing at my bad luck I murmured, "Yes, alright," and hung up. By now the guard had arrived from the rear driving cab of the loco wanting to know what had happened. I told him what the 'bobby' had said, but neither of us could see the slightest sign of any heated axle boxes. I followed the appropriate signals for going inside the goods loop and we trundled down to the far end of the loop where the examiner was already waiting for us. He took details of the engine, my name and depot, and then started his examination of the train. The guard and myself walked round with him, and at the end of twenty minutes he was as puzzled as ourselves, but gave us clearance to get on our way. Later I learned that there had been a 'short' on some of the detector circuits. To set the record straight however, I must admit that the equipment is a marvellous gadget and can save the operating department a lot of time and money.

I wonder if the railway industry in Britain has grown too big for itself, with perhaps its employees losing that most important incentive of all, the love of the job for its own sake. There is always continual talk of, and sometimes threats to close down, unprofitable lines. This in itself is sound common-sense, but the answer to the question, "Why are they unprofitable?", hardly seems to be heard above the clamour for more and more increased fares which have grown steadily prohibitive to the public while the services offered seem to have steadily declined. I feel sure that a reduction in charges, coupled with a more reasonable time-table, would bring the public back to the railways. From an economic point of view alone, they are desperately needed.

Over the past two or three years un-sociable hours have become a popular conversation topic, especially when wage agreements are negotiated or discussed. This is particularly true of engine crews and track staff; but then, they have always worked these awkward times which disrupt family life. The social life of the enginemen, or rather, the lack of it, has always been a black back-drop in the history of the railways.

A roster with booking-on for duty at 3.00 a.m. usually means a crewman leaving his comfortable bed at about 2 o'clock. You may not think that there is anything unusual about this—most people get up about an hour before they are due at work. But I have, as many others, ridden to work in the teeth of a gale, with the rain slashing down heavens hard. Believe me, at that time in the morning such foul weather always seems to be twice as rough as in the friendlier light of day. I arrive at work with water squelching in my shoes and my trousers saturated from the knees down, then as I go in the drivers' lobby, some bright spark will pipe up, "Is it raining?"

"No. I've been under the water column for a quick shower " What else can one say?

I am now faced with the gloomy prospect of starting at least eight hours of duty with feet wet through and legs as cold as ice. Only the thought of a night out with my wife has somewhat managed to softened my discomfort. I recall one such time.

I had planned my day well. Knocking off at 11.00 a.m. I would cycle home to a spot of breakfast-cum-lunch, followed by bed for a few hours before going out. At least, that was the theory. This particular morning I was due to relieve a train for Willesden from Carlisle at Basford Hall South Junction. Diesel hauled, it was due at 3.45 a.m., but after an hour and a quarter of impatient waiting and cussing on my part, it had still not arrived. At 5.30 I rang control and asked where the heck it was. "Anytime now," replied the controller. "We have it passing Warrington at 5.15." I did a quick calculation and figured that for a fully fitted goods train there would be at the most, thirty-five minutes running time.

It was a quarter past six when the English Electric type '4' hauled train eventually arrived, the driver explaining that he had been inside the loop at Acton Bridge and had stood at Hartford Junction for some considerable time. This standing was necessary to allow the more important night liner and car trains to overtake.

I went through the usual formalities of taking over and eventually received clearance at 6.30 a.m. The road was clear right through to Stafford, which for a goods train was unusual, to say the the least. Right on through Lichfield we powered, turning on to the slow line at Tamworth before coming to a state of rest at Atherstone at 8 a.m. Three hours to go and my day's work would be finished. I requested relief at either Nuneaton or Rugby and was told that this would be arranged. Half an hour later we left Atherstone, still on the slow line, with green signals all the way to

Nuneaton and me wondering why we had been delayed so long at Atherstone. At Nuneaton we were given a clear road straight through, with obviously no relief there, so we continued to Rugby, arriving at 9.20 a.m. I enquired about my relief only to be told that there was not a 'single' man available. A little angry and sarcastic, I said that a 'married' man would do, but after a few heated words I reluctantly agreed to go as far as Bletchley—"But no further."

We pulled out of Rugby at 10 o'clock, and I maintained a steady 45 miles per hour, with a good path all the way. On arrival at Bletchley, by now 45 minutes into overtime, I still waited to be relieved in order that I could return to Crewe; my enquiry about a relief drew the same reply as at Rugby. My explanations that I had commenced duty at 3 a.m. fell on deaf ears, and I was sorely tempted to shut the diesel down and leave the train, but this has never been my way of doing things, so once more the reluctant hero, I proceeded to Willesden on the slow line, arriving at 2.15 p.m. Lo and behold, there was my relief crew waiting!

If I could have caught a train there and then I might have been able to get back to Crewe about two hours later. As it was I had to catch the 3.05 to Liverpool from Euston, and it was on this train that I met the dear old lady in the restaurant car (referred to in Chapter XIII). When I finally arrived back in Crewe at half past five it was too late to have our 'night on the town', especially with a compulsory twelve hours rest period before having to be in fine fettle at 4.30 the following morning ready for work. My wife was then, as always, very understanding, and she cast her eyes heavenwards and said with disappointment in her voice, "Who would be an engine driver's wife." Who indeed. Perhaps when you have read about the following incident you will agree that her tolerance has passed a sterner test than most.

My wife and I were married on Saturday, 3rd September, 1947, and at 3 o'clock on the Sunday morning there came a thunderous knocking at our front door. After just twelve hours of married bliss I crawled bleary-eyed out of bed and, as far as possible under the circumstances, politely asked what the blazes was going on. A voice called out, "Do the Stewarts live here?"

"Well, they were doing their best until you came along."

"I have come from the shed", the voice answered, and I've been asked to tell you to report for duty as soon as you can."

My reply was swift and to the point, and is definitely not repeatable! However I did report for duty the following Wednesday, when the foreman admitted having sent for me, only realising after the call boy had gone on his errand, that I was on special leave. His final comment "I hope that I didn't inconvenience you" must surely rank as one of the great under-statements!

Both in my days as an engine driver for British Rail and later for the A4 Society, I have always been impressed by the enthusiasm and knowledge of youngsters, the railwaymen (and women) of tomorrow, the enthusiasts for all time. They are every bit as knowledgeable about diesels and electrics as my generation was about steam locomotives. What is more, they have absorbed the traditions of the days of steam and discuss in learned terms about such wide ranging topics as the relative merits of one locomotive against another, the procedure for isolating a defective cylinder, the operation and function of the Automatic Warning System etc. etc. They are thoroughly on the ball, as the saying goes; in fact I would say that they are 'on the right lines'.

Many times, in response to impassioned pleas, I have taken them onto the footplate to give a driver's eye-view, so to speak, and have taken the opportunity to warn of the hazards of the line. I have been rewarded by their looks of awe as they have come to realise the difficulties of a driver. I just hope that my messages of safety have got across to them; I am fairly sure that they have.

The continued recruitment of trainees from the ranks of these young enthusiasts can, I am sure, only be of great benefit to British Rail in the future. With their awareness of the problems of others within the industry, and with an increasingly encouraged and educated knowledge of the thousands of theories and practices essential to the efficient running of a railway, the priceless incentive of job satisfaction, present manifestly absent in British Rail, will return.

Late in 1967 my footplate career was nearing its end, my enthusiasm and interest for the railway life sadly beginning to wane. Management had displayed a peculiar lack of sensitivity for the steam locomotive footplatemen during the transition to diesels and electrics, and at this time, many of my colleagues at Crewe, like those in other depots throughout the country, felt the same way as myself; few on them would have hesitated for a moment had they been offered a chance to change their jobs.

My feelings of unsettlement and dis-satisfaction burned so strongly inside me that my wife agreed that I should look elsewhere. Accordingly, we applied for a public house managership, but the particular house for which we applied became vacant while we were on our Canadian holiday, and so we missed the chance. However, I kept the application in with the brewery, and in August, 1969, I was invited to an interview with the brewery manager.

This was the point of no return. I had been with the railway for thirty-two years, and now, when faced with the decision about whether or not to change jobs, I began to have doubts. It was a case of 'Speak now, or forever hold your peace'. I thought the advice I had received from my father and George Whalley when I had wondered about moving to Crewe, so after my wife and I had discussed the pros and cons with the manager, and both of us had thought deeply on the matter, I made the bold decision to accept the tenacy of the 'Sebastopol Inn', Moor Road, Chorley, Lancashire.

We moved in two days before Christmas, 1969, totally inexperienced, and remembering that the brewery had warned us that the job would be especially hard work at that time of the year. He wasn't joking! The trade was hotting up prior to the real Christmas rush, and on Christmas Eve we both felt that the entire population of Chorley (or was it Lancashire?) had descended upon us. For myself, I have never been as tired at the end of a day's work as I was then.

During our probationary period we relied heavily upon the help of Jack Kinlock, and I do not think we could have survived without him. Indeed he more than proved his worth, especially to my wife, when, during the hectic New Year's Eve celebrations I collapsed with pneumonia. After only one week in residence my wife was left as a team of one, and so she remained for the next six weeks, working herself to a frazzle. Jack, during this difficult period, did his own job with a local firm during the day, and helped behind the bar at night. To you, Jack, our sincerest thanks, for all you did for us.

We have settled down nice and comfortably since then, but for the first twelve months I had severe misgivings about what I had done. I yearned for the days and nights, thundering across England on the iron rails, a mighty engine at my command. I missed the company of my mates most of all though, and longed for someone to call in and talk of Crewe and the railways. But I survived.

Old friends and colleauges drop in fairly regularly now and I keep up to date with the wanderings and workings of my 'Blue Lady', now she is out on the main line with regular steam excursions in the North West and Yorkshire. Indeed if you find yourself with a spare half-hour and are near Chorley, please drop in for a pint and a natter. I'll look forward to seeing you.

I cannot close this book without saying what a great pleasure and privilege it was for me to work with and know the footplate men of British Rail. For my many happy years among them I wish to place on record my tribute to engine men everywhere.

You are the very foundation stone of the railways of this great country. I am proud to have known you.

Cheerio, chaps Mind how you go, watch the signals, and

KEEP ON THE RIGHT LINES

★   ★   ★